• PS-850 •

BREEDING AND CARING FOR
CHINCHILLAS

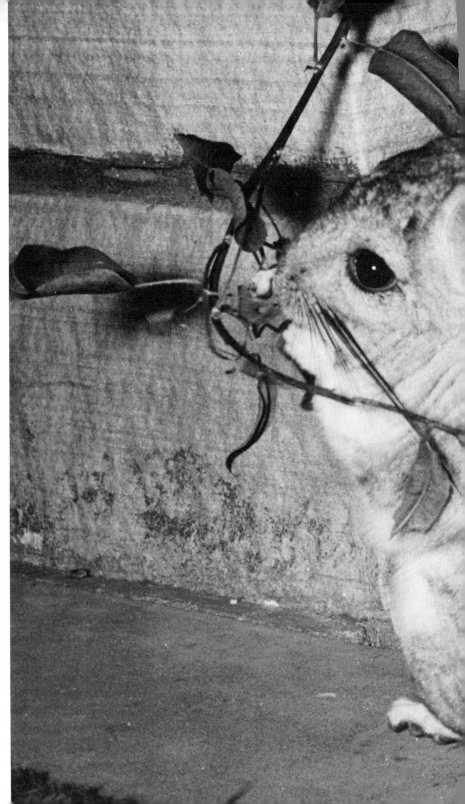

BREEDING AND CARING FOR
CHINCHILLAS

EGON MÖSSLACHER

Contents

Becoming more popular all the time, chinchillas have much to recommend them. They're clean and cuddly and interesting, and they respond well to affection.

PREFACE

Although chinchillas are relatively new introductions to the pet market, they have long been bred for their pelts. This may sound cruel to some chin owners, but it is a fact of life. Please remember that the modern chinchilla is a domestic animal to some extent, much like the large number of foxes, minks, and nutria that are selectively bred, cared for, and commercially farmed in thousands of fur ranches around the world. Without the fur farms you probably would not have your pet chinchilla, as the original pet stock—and much of the present pet stock still—was derived from culls and other animals unwanted by chinchilla pelt farmers.

Virtually all we know about caring for, feeding, and breeding chinchillas is through decades of research by chinchilla ranchers. This groundwork cost them decades in time and millions of dollars in money—and it is yours virtually free to use with your pet chin.

This book is written by an experienced chinchilla rancher who has modified for the pet field his extensive knowledge of the care and raising of chinchillas. The sections on selective breeding of chins are especially important to pet owners as they provide guidelines that will help in establishing uniform color varieties in pet chins that will make them even more important pets.

So remember just where your pet chins come from and why they are available in the first place. Chins make cute, enjoyable pets, but at least for now this is only a sideline in the chinchilla industry. Be thankful for the knowledge you are getting from the sweat and wallets of the chinchilla farms of the last 40 years, and be glad that their culls are now the forefathers of a new generation of pets to be loved and protected by thousands of contented owners.

INTRODUCTION

I made costly mistakes due to inexperience when I first started breeding chinchillas back in 1958. Back then all of us who got into this totally new field of breeding chinchillas had little real experience in this area. Those breeders who set out to establish their operation in a systematic and determined way, who constantly improved the quality of their animals through selective breeding, who could not be deterred by setbacks, were in the end inevitably successful. Those breeders who took up breeding chinchillas in order to reap a quick profit and disregarded the basic principles of sound animal husbandry and those who sought shortcuts in daily maintenance invariably did not last. The causes of most failures can be found in the disregard of sound animal management practices.

I have attempted in this book to maintain simplicity of style and content. I have deliberately shied away from highly technical discussions on genetics, line-breeding, mutations, and veterinary medicine since I know how confusing these topics can be. What is of paramount importance to every chinchilla breeder is a healthy breeding stock, excellent fur quality, love and dedication for the animal, an understanding and appreciation of its characteristics, patience and perseverance, and—last but certainly not least—the best possible care and maintenance.

Even though chinchillas became introduced to the pet-loving public more or less as a by-product of the animals' use as providers of fur, the chinchillas sold in pet shops were in almost every case bred specifically to be pets—they were never intended to become pelts.

If you learn from my experience and adhere to my recommendations you will without doubt be successful in breeding chinchillas—I am absolutely convinced of that. I sincerely hope that you will be able to take full advantage of the details presented in this book, and I wish you every success as a chinchilla breeder.

Egon Mösslacher

1. Characteristics of Chinchillas

Chinchillas are peaceful, small hystricomorph rodents that do not disturb anyone. Their dense fur, long whiskers, and long, bushy tail are distinctive. When threatened or pursued they rely on their agility, their teeth, and their ability to shed patches of fur. When frightened or captured they tend to give off a pungent odor similar to that of scorched almonds. This scent is sprayed from a gland located just inside the anus. In addition, females have a further defense mechanism—they stand up on their hind legs and, lightning fast, excrete urine at a presumed attacker.

The loss of fur patches is of understandable significance to the chinchilla keeper. Shed fur or fur ripped out due to clumsy handling of the animal causes bare patches where the skin shines through. It takes about six to eight weeks for the patches to be covered with fur again, and it may take several months for the fur to grow to the same length as the surrounding areas. Of course, the loss of a little fur is of no real consequence to the animal itself, as it is a painless natural method of defense, but it does make an unsightly animal and never fails to worry the owner the first time it happens.

The danger of hair loss is particularly likely when an animal becomes frightened or is being handled. In order to avoid this problem, chinchillas are best handled by their tail or ears, a practice that may seem somewhat unusual to a beginning chinchilla breeder.

Chinchillas are not aggressive by nature. They will use their teeth only when handled, touched, or held clumsily. They do not like to be petted without being firmly restrained, although they can sometimes be scratched under their chin. Most pets soon adapt to some handling and even enjoy being scratched, but this may take some time. As more and more pet-bred chins become available it is likely that their offspring will become more accustomed to handling and friendlier and friendlier.

Chinchillas need a daily bath . . . a sand bath, that is! This serves to keep up their well-being as well as promoting cleanliness and beauty of the fur.

Chinchillas, like most rodents, are mostly nocturnal (active at night) animals. During the day in nature they sleep in hollows, caves, and other hiding places. With the onset of dusk they become active and start looking for food. Because these animals are crepuscular (active at dusk) and nocturnal they must be kept in breeding rooms that are in quiet locations so that their rest is not disturbed during the day.

Chinchillas are very clean animals. When kept under proper conditions in a well-ventilated area they do not omit an offensive odor. They are, however, sensitive to various pests, particularly mice, dogs, and cats, which must be kept away from them. Their fur does not harbor such parasites as fleas or lice, presumedly because it is so extremely dense.

A somewhat less desirable characteristic—more like a vice—is what is known as fur biting. Similar to chickens that peck each other's feathers, some chinchillas gnaw occasionally on their own fur or on that of others around them. More on this important subject later.

Chinchillas are running and jumping animals that move about with lightning-fast agility. Once they have escaped from their cage they are not very easy to recapture. They are also curious animals and will gnaw on just about anything, including furniture and electrical wiring, if given a chance.

When chinchillas vocalize, their sounds resemble a frightened chirp and peep or an angry cackling sound when annoyed. They can also emit warning sounds, which sound like "kee-kee-kee." Hissing and growling are not known to occur.

The male is often referred to as a buck, but there is no standard name for the female, although many keepers of course call her a doe. Chinchillas do not build nests. The young are usually born during the early daylight hours. At birth they have already short fur and their eyes are functional. Their teeth are already present, and they grow continuously. For that reason chinchillas must *always* be provided with something to chew on, such as chewing stones (pumice rock), hazelnut branches, or similar items. Chinchillas can be kept either in pairs (monogamously) or in groups (polygamously, one buck and several does).

The outstanding characteristic of chinchillas is their fur, which is unmatched by any other commercially farmed fur-bearing animal. It is silky, dense, and unusually light and soft. In its "agouti pattern" (named after another South American rodent, the agouti) it has tricolored markings designated the lower zone (undercoat), band, and veil (clouding). Protruding for only a few millimeters beyond the undercoat of the fur are special guard hairs or "deck" hairs (also referred to as "king's hairs"). These guard hairs provide special elasticity to the mature pelt. The abdominal region of the pelt usually does not have the agouti pattern, instead being white to light gray.

2. General Care

HOW TO HANDLE CHINCHILLAS

When breeding animals it is very important to respond properly to the peculiarities of a particular animal. When keeping chinchillas this becomes the First Commandment. It is in this area that the most serious and far-reaching mistakes are being made, because too often breeders become complacent and tend to cater more to themselves than to the needs of their charges.

A breeder must have a steady hand. If he is nervous and hasty by nature the animals will sense this and become equally nervous. He must also have lots of love and affection for his animals, as well as lots of patience. Experience has shown that many chinchilla breeding attempts have failed because these essential elements were lacking in a breeder.

It is very important to talk to an animal before you touch it. A calm voice tends to have a pacifying effect on a frightened animal, particularly on a chinchilla. Every animal should occasionally be picked up and held gently. When you take a pregnant female out of its cage, DO NOT pick it up by the tail and DO NOT let it dangle in mid-air; this can lead to a spontaneous abortion.

Chinchillas will only bite when frightened and cornered. Such a bite can inflict a deep and rather painful

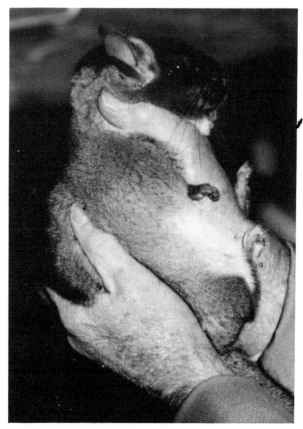

Illustrated here is one of the ways to hold a chinchilla properly; the main idea is to achieve firm but gentle support for the body.

wound, but it is never very serious. Novice breeders will notice that newly acquired animals are shy and restless; they have to adapt to their new surroundings and to their new owner. This is a natural and expected process. Beginners have to adhere strictly to the instructions passed on to them when they received the animals. For instance, experience has shown over and over again that a cage must never be placed in the middle of a room!

An example: Some time ago I set up a small breeding facility for a beginner; it consisted of one buck and several females. The room being used was suitable for this number of animals. I placed the cage in one corner. The new owner thought he was doing his animals a favor when, at the onset of the cold season, he placed the cage in the middle of the room. The consequence of this was that the animals could now be watched and looked at from all sides, and they no longer had the protection afforded them in the corner. As things tend to go, relatives and friends all had to inspect the newly arrived, expensive, and exotic animals, so they never got any peace and quiet. Finally they became so frightened that they would race madly around their cage whenever the door to the room was opened. In their state of constant anxiety the animals then started to chew on their own furs. Such animals under constant harassment will of course not bear any young at all.

Another bad habit of novice breeders is that they tend to mistake their chinchillas for lap dogs! They take them to bed and offer them all sorts of tidbits, such as raisins and peanuts. Peanuts can be offered occasionally to chinchillas, as indeed they can to many other animals. With commercial "delicacies" it has to be remembered that they must not have been treated with chemicals. Snacks tend to inhibit normal feeding and ultimately can lead to obese animals. Obese males can have difficulties mating, and females may have difficulties during labor. So if you plan on breeding your chins, limit the snacks and stick to balanced chinchilla diets.

Because chins may bite and shed fur when grabbed, many commercial producers recommend picking them up by either the ears or the tail. If done carefully this does not seem to bother the chins and they do not become upset. Be sure that the animal is at rest before catching it. The ears are carefully pinched together—gently—to lift the animal up. NEVER leave it dangling, but immediately put an arm under it for support, then hold it with the hands. When picking up a chin by its tail, be sure to grab as close to the root as possible, otherwise you might break it or the tip might come off. Provide support as soon as possible. If the tail is accidentally damaged it will usually heal eventually.

THE BREEDING ROOM

Anyone wanting to breed chinchillas has to resolve the room problem first. There is no point in getting the animals and then not being able to provide them with proper accommodations. Experience continues to show that to this day there are still people keeping chinchillas—which have been bought for a lot of money—under less than marginal conditions. Good animal husbandry requires proper housing for the animals.

The room designated for chinchillas must be sufficiently large, dry and well-ventilated, but it must also be draft-free and have facilities for heating during the cold season. The heat source must be located outside the breeding room! Many a breeder has lost his entire animal stock through smoke and carbon monoxide poisoning by not observing this simple and self-explanatory guideline. The room must also be lockable and thus not accessible to everyone around. Ideally, it should be in a quiet location and not directly adjacent to or exposed to noise pollution such as work shops, busy streets, playgrounds, and similar places. Constant airport noise is also undesirable and damaging. It is also advantageous if the windows of the breeding room are facing east so that there is access to morning sun and the mid-day heat during the summer is kept out. The floor must be covered with a plastic material that can be cleaned easily, but special care must be given so that moisture does not accumulate on the floor, which can lead to the development of fungus. If kept in a building outside the house, the walls must be properly insulated with Styrofoam or a similar material.

A breeding room for chinchillas must not become a

general store room for house and garden. Other animals (such as rabbits!) must also be kept out—pest species (rats and mice) as well as cats and dogs must be prevented from entering the breeding room and disturbing the chins.

The following types of rooms and facilities are generally NOT suited for keeping and breeding chinchillas: damp basements, attics without proper insulation against heat and cold, garages, laundry rooms, rooms frequently used by people (kitchens, living and bed rooms, work shops, offices), broom closets, store rooms, heating rooms, bathrooms.

When considering the breeding room question, it is important to remember to also consider the need for additional space to accommodate the anticipated young and older animals retired from breeding.

The breeding room must have provisions for heating. The preferred temperature during the cold season is 15 to 18°C maximum (59 to 65°F). Juveniles could be kept in unheated rooms, but the drinking water must never be permitted to freeze over. During hot summer months the temperature MUST NOT EXCEED 28 to 30°C (82 to 86°F). If the ambient temperature is over 30°C, windows and shutters must be kept closed during the day, and kept open at night until dawn. Chinchillas originally may be from a tropical country (Chile), but they are from a high altitude, cold climate.

Breeding room decorations such as flowers and indoor plants must be omitted, since on the one hand they remove oxygen from the air and on the other hand they increase the level of humidity in the room.

The importance of basic prerequisites for housing and maintenance can be demonstrated by the following example:

I was asked to see a breeder who had encountered a number of mortalities among his stock that he could not

Adult chinchillas are appealing—but baby chinchillas like this youngster are almost irresistible!

explain. When I entered the breeding room I immediately noticed that the air was very sticky and the room poorly ventilated. When examining the droppings underneath the various cages I saw that all the animals were ill. Some had diarrhea, while others suffered from constipation. The breeder insisted that he had done everything recommended for keeping chinchillas. Consequently, as far as he was concerned it had to be some unknown epidemic that had suddenly occurred. Since I had heard such utterances from breeders many times before, I was unimpressed and extended my inspection to the feed. There I saw that the hay was tough and totally unsuitable. It originally came from an orchard where there was short grass (often referred to as "sow grass") growing underneath the fruit trees. Moreover, calcium tablets packed in aluminum foil to protect them against humidity had become so damp that the entire package could be crushed with only slight pressure. All this was evidence enough that the room was totally unsuitable for breeding chinchillas. The cause of the mortalities was therefore not to be found in the animals themselves, but rather in the seriously deficient accommodations and inadequate care. This diagnosis was confirmed by a veterinarian who had also been consulted.

In the final analysis, it is strongly advisable for any beginning chinchilla breeder to seek the advice and counsel of an experienced breeder before he sets up his new venture. It will save the novice much aggravation, disappointment, and money.

CAGES AND EQUIPMENT

Breeding cages for chinchillas must be made of galvanized, point-welded wire mesh. Those made of wood or cheap chicken wire are unsuitable.

Nowadays it has become common practice to keep the breeding animals in cages without a wire bottom so that the animals are running directly on wood shavings placed in the bottom cage tray. Apart from the fact that it is difficult to obtain suitable wood shavings, difficult to store this material, and then difficult to dispose of it again after use, there is also a risk that these shavings could come from stained, glued, or lacquered wood. Since the animals tend to chew on wood shavings, this has in the past lead to some fatal poisoning problems.

Running the animals on a wire mesh bottom instead of on wood shavings enhances the cleanliness of both the cage and the animals. I always run my animals on a wire mesh bottom, and when this is kept clean I have never noticed any disadvantages with this method. All left-over food and the droppings fall into the tray below. This then facilitates close monitoring of the condition of the droppings, and the copulatory plug can also be eas-

A rectangular metal cage constructed of galvanized wire is the best type of housing unit for chinchillas. Such cages are easily obtainable at pet shops, as are all of the incidental pieces of equipment that are used in day-to-day chinchilla care.

ily found. Thus the animals' quarters are always clean. I usually put sawdust in the tray and replace it once a week. Newspaper can also be used. The tray should be of a sliding type so it can be removed for washing and brushing with a wire brush.

I have found the most suitable individual cage dimensions to be 60 cm long, 60 cm deep (front to back), and 55 cm high (24 x 24 x 22 inches); small variations are inconsequential. Due to lack of space, many breeders are now using smaller and smaller cages without considering the implications on the well-being and reproduction of the animals. The minimum space requirements are quite definitely a cage of not less than 50 cm in length, 50 cm in width, and 40 cm in height (20 x 20 x 16 inches). Anyone establishing a breeding colony of chinchillas must also give immediate consideration to cages for keeping the young. These can be smaller than the breeding cages but must not fall below 40 cm in length, 40 cm in width, and 35 cm in height (16 x 16 x 14 inches).

Inside the cage is the dust bath covered by a resting board (perch). There can be different types of dust bath tubs. Some breeders use bowls or basins for the sand bath, some prefer large cans modified and cut to size, metal buckets, baby bath tubs, or similar items. Many pet keepers find a large glass jar excellent.

Next to the door along the front wire of the cage there must be a clamp or ring to secure the water bottle and a hay hopper. The latter can also be attached directly to the door. I prefer to use glass bowls for food; these can be placed inside the cage directly through a small opening in one of the wire panels.

Finally, there must be a metal card holder attached to the cage for keeping records of breeding. These cards are used to record details on births, sex, identifying tattoo marks, litter details, and litter size.

The details of the layout of an ideal cage can be visualized as follows, using a plan I follow. The perch or resting board covers the dust bath container. On the outside is a sturdy wire lever that is used to raise the perch and thus open the dust bath. It is recommended that the edges of the perch be reinforced thin pliable sheet metal in order to prevent the animals from chewing on them. When closing the dust bath it is important to make sure that the lid fits tightly so that juveniles cannot slip into the closed bath and strangle. The feed container, preferably a glass or pottery bowl glazed on the inside, is slightly elevated. The food bowl is slid into the cage directly through a small opening made just for that purpose in the wire panel; a movable wire can prevent the bowl from being pushed out by the animal.

Chinchillas enjoying a dust bath in a cat litter pan; in choosing a receptacle to use as a dust bath area for chinchillas, make sure that the sides of the enclosure are high enough to prevent wholesale scattering of the dust.

The bowl should be placed slightly higher than the floor so that the animals will not sit in it and get the food soiled with urine or droppings. The hay hopper is also attached well above the floor, often near the door.

Try to avoid having to open the cage for bathing, feeding, and watering. This is of paramount importance in breeding both because the animals should be disturbed as little as possible and because it saves time and effort. These factors can be decisive when a large number of animals have to be cared for.

NEST BOXES

It frequently happens that chinchilla females avoid their own young, so during the first few hours and days of their lives the newborn are not kept sufficiently warm. This problem can be eliminated with a heated nest box. A nest box is attached to the inside of the door about three or four days (up to eight days) prior to the expected birth of a litter. The heat source inside the box consists of 15-watt incandescent light bulb. NEVER use a larger light bulb! This would overheat the young and cause irreparable damage, possibly even death. The nest box remains in place for up to three weeks after the birth of a litter. In centrally heated facilities a nest box is not necessary.

The nest box is made of wood, simply constructed, and can be made by the breeder. Many chinchilla breeders utilize a very simple closed nest box that is just placed inside the cage. During mating and other lively activities of the animals this box often gets pushed around and even turned over, which can easily lead to injuries or even death of the newborn. A properly designed, heated nest box attached to the outside of the cage eliminates this danger. The box should be large enough for the mother and her young but not too roomy. The bottom should be double, with the light bulb in this false bottom where it cannot be touched by the chin. Entry is through a hole in one side—the hole must of course be large enough for the mother to go in and out, but she will enlarge it slightly if necessary. If at all possible, the front of the box should be hinged for access to the young and for cleaning. Simple but dependable wire hangers on the back attach it to the cage. The electric cord to the bulb must of course be outside the cage.

Nest boxes made of sheet metal must be avoided under all circumstances! Sheet metal is cold and cools off

A correctly constructed nest box, showing how the electrical cord is kept entirely *outside* the cage. The nest box is attached to the wire cage by wire hangers; the front of the nest box is hinged.

immediately during a power failure (or when it is not turned on). Moreover, humidity tends to precipitate on the metal walls, which then leads to oxidation (rust!).

The females in my breeding facility use nest boxes regularly. This then prevents litter mortalities due to cold exposure and also provides a good refuge for the female to dry her fur, which eliminates the danger of mammary gland inflammation. In cold situations without a nest box it is quite possible for the first young to die while the mother is still giving birth to the second young and unable to attend the first.

3. Nutrition

Chinchilla food pellets became available in my area in 1958, the year when I started breeding chinchillas. At that time pellets were considered to be only a supplementary food, while the main diet consisted of the traditional types of grain and a mixture of wheat bran, wheat germ, dry yeast, dietary calcium, and ground corn. Such a diet required constant vigilance to maintain the correct dietary component ratio for proper droppings consistency so that constipation and diarrhea were avoided. This was not always easy to do! When chinchilla breeding became more popular a pelleted chinchilla diet also became more popular. Today the composition and quality of these pellets is so advanced that they form the main part of a chinchilla diet. Therefore, the basic nutrition of chinchillas is really no longer a problem—it now consists generally of pellets, hay, and water.

In spite of the improved quality of chinchilla pellets, I continue to use a mixed diet, which I have managed to improve more and more over the years. This is because in my experience I have noticed that even the best quality pellets are nutritionally inadequate to obtain consistently adequate progeny and avoid difficulties while raising the young. I contribute my excellent breeding results solely to this diet—pellets plus mixed food—because healthy and strong young are the very foundation of successful chinchilla breeding.

This is my proven dietary regimen:

Main (Evening) Feeding
1 tablespoon pellets per animal
1 bottle fresh drinking water
1 handful hay (new harvest, freshly cut)

Morning Feeding
½ tablespoon food mixture
1 bottle fresh drinking water
1 handful hay

In addition, each animal receives one piece of dried bread (thumb-size) and may receive a wedge of apple.

The food mixture consists of the following:
3 kg wheat bran, coarse
3 kg oats
3 kg barley
3 kg wheat
1 kg millet
½ kg linseed
½ kg dietary calcium, commercial grade
½ kg feed salt, commercial grade
200 g fennel
200 g skimmed milk powder

Furthermore, I add the following herbs to the diet mixture, ground up between my fingers:
3 heaped tablespoons chamomile
3 heaped tablespoons hip
2 heaped tablespoons peppermint
1 heaped tablespoon sage
1 heaped tablespoon mallow
½ heaped tablespoon St. John's wort

When all this is thoroughly mixed together it will give about 15 kg, sufficient for 100 animals for eight to ten weeks. It should be stored dry and cool so that it retains a suitable degree of freshness. If only a small number of animals are to be fed, the mixture can be prepared with proportionately smaller amounts of ingredients (⅛‘¼, ⅓, or ¼ of each).

If a female is nursing young it must get an additional ⅓ tablespoon of mixture for the morning feeding. Young that are being weaned off the female should be given about half a ration (of pellets and mixture) until their fourth month. They should receive this amount in the morning and evening; that is, half a tablespoon per animal. Strict compliance with these recommendations usually assures well-developed young.

In addition, all animals must receive weekly vitamin supplements, primarily vitamins D and C. It is important that vitamin supplements are stored in a dry location and humidity (which softens the tablets) is kept out completely. Dietary calcium supplements are also recommended. During the summer chinchillas should be offered two or three dandelion or hazel leaves daily as additional vitamin supplements and to promote lactation in nursing females. Apple wedges do this in winter.

With this varied diet mixture supported by appropriate animal husbandry procedures and proper hygiene, I have never had any fur biters or cases of constipation, especially when new litters are born.

A final word of warning to the beginning chinchilla breeder: heed the feeding instructions given when acquiring your animals from the vendor. Well-meaning advice or "secret recipes" passed on a bit too eagerly from other breeders should be categorically rejected.

RABBIT PELLETS

The possible use of rabbit pellets requires a stern warning! Chinchilla breeders, like many people, are sometimes inclined to save on the wrong thing. Since chinchilla pellets may seem to be too expensive to some, they use instead rabbit pellets, which are considerably cheaper. This may indeed work reasonably well for a while. Yet, sooner or later the inevitable always happens—fewer young and finally none at all! The reason for this is obvious to any clear-thinking individual: rabbit pellets are heavily fortified with hormones for the primary purpose of meat production. Therefore, it is not surprising to find that chinchillas fed on rabbit pellets will get too fat within six months. Bucks become lethargic, and fewer and fewer females get pregnant. Mixing rabbit and chinchilla pellets must also be rejected on similar grounds. The bottom line of all this is that rabbit pellets do not provide a real financial saving. On the contrary, they are usually a very expensive "short cut."

TIDBITS

Never offer any tidbits such as dry bread or pieces of apple outside regular feeding times. Never offer tidbits to one animal and not the others. Chinchillas are very sensitive and become more so when other animals get preferential treatment. Novices sometimes consider this to be a complicating factor when keeping chinchillas. This, however, is not the case.

APPLE VINEGAR

Breeding animals that are reluctant to feed, as well as those that are physiologically weakened such as females after having given birth, can be offered drinking water to which some pure apple vinegar (cider vinegar) has been added. This tends to stimulate appetite and so helps the animal to regain its normal weight. The usual dosage of vinegar is about 10 drops per water bottle for one animal per day. This corresponds to about half a teaspoon per 250 ml of water. Most chinchillas eagerly accept the vinegar additive in their drinking water. It is given until an improvment in the animal's condition is observed.

Giving apple vinegar with drinking water also has been shown to be beneficial for pregnant females. They usually do not encounter difficulties while giving birth, especially young females in their first pregnancy. The vinegar additive also prevents loss of lactation in nursing females. Apple vinegar is commonly available from health food stores and supermarkets.

FEEDING TIMES

It is generally known that pets and domestic animals have a very well-defined sense of time, especially as far as feeding times are concerned. I have observed the same in chinchillas. Therefore, it is very important they always are fed and watered at the same time. Delays of several hours can cause convulsions in some chins when they are finally fed. Some chinchillas even become fur biters if put on an irregular feeding schedule. I advise every chinchilla breeder to set aside a certain time slot each evening for the main feeding and then rigidly stick to it.

There are also different opinions in regard to the main feeding. Some breeders insist it must be given in the morning, while others believe the evening hours are more appropriate. Since the chinchilla is a nocturnal animal and most of its activities occur at night, I firmly believe they should start out their nocturnal activities with a substantial meal. For that reason—confirmed by years of experience—the evening feeding should be the main meal for chinchillas. The morning feeding then becomes a so-called "topping off" feeding as described above, including pieces of dry bread and apple wedges.

I am not convinced that so-called fasting days, as practiced by some chinchilla breeders, serve any useful purpose.

Chinchillas are not hard to keep well if attention is paid to their basic needs—and they reward their keepers many times over for the attention given them.

DROPPINGS AS A BAROMETER OF HEALTH

Droppings (feces) are the barometer of health of chinchillas! Therefore, the breeder has to check them daily. This is best done during the morning feeding or during the morning inspection if the animals are fed only in the evening. Experienced breeders need only a quick glance at the feces accumulation, but a novice will have to spend a bit more time on this very important duty. Consistency and appearance of the droppings are of greatest importance. This will tell the breeder whether his animals are healthy, if there is a health problem, and even whether the animals suffer from a particular deficiency because of an unsuitable diet.

If the droppings are getting smaller, a pinch (tip of a knife blade) of Karlsbad salt is added to the drinking water. If the droppings are soft, the amount of food is maintained and Terramycin (oxytetracycline) is added to the drinking water, ½ teaspoon of powder per 250 ml water, properly mixed; the water bottle is not refilled until the animals have taken all the water. When young chinchillas are weaned off their mother there is a tendency toward over-feeding, often resulting in loose droppings. This can also be corrected with Terramycin.

PROBLEM DROPPINGS

Droppings from a chinchilla with a completely healthy digestive tract are relatively plump, oval to rounded, and of uniform size. It is important that the droppings do not have hollow cavities when broken apart and do not contain undigested hay remnants (fibers). The color of normal droppings (when dry) ranges from olive green to dark brown. The feces of a normal healthy animal have smooth surfaces (not rough!).

Droppings that are long, thin, bent, and have a rough surface occur in animals with digestive problems due to an inadequate diet. Such animals are still normally active, but they usually do not breed. *Treatment:* lots of rough, dry hay, also oat straw . . . (caution: there is a risk of fungus!).

Small, dry, rough droppings indicate a serious health problem. Usually droppings like these are already accompanied by a loss of condition. If there is no immediate proper treatment the animal will invariably die. *Treatment:* Apple vinegar and high quality hay often produce a remarkably quick improvement. Chinchillas with droppings like these also suffer from a loss of appetite. This can also be corrected with fruit vinegar. If animals in this condition have come from another establishment, it is advisable to add suitable dosages of Karlsbad salt to their drinking water before any treatment is initiated. The Karlsbad salt facilitates the establishment of a suitable intestinal flora. Experience has shown if this is unsuccessful the animal has already sustained liver damage that usually can not be corrected.

One more type of dropping must be mentioned here which facilitates recognition of an imminent case of diarrhea. It is similar to normal droppings but is colored grass-green, is glossy, and is slimy. It can easily be squashed between two fingers. The recommended treatment is Terramycin given in drinking water and a normal diet, as before. This type of dropping is often seen in subadult chinchillas and is due to over-feeding.

HAY: THE MAIN DIET COMPONENT

The main diet of chinchillas is hay. The most suitable hay is that from unfertilized meadows or other grassy areas. Hay must never be too fresh. By this I mean that hay must not be fed immediately after it has been brought in from the meadows. The reason for this is that the fermentation has not yet been completed. This also applies to hay fed to cattle and horses. *Any suggestion to the contrary is wrong.* Fresh hay can cause serious

Closeup of a chinchilla about to begin its dust bath. Chinchillas take eagerly to bathing themselves in dust baths, but if a young animal is prevented from bathing for a protracted period it might lose its inclination to bathe.

A female chinchilla enjoying her dust bath, as the flying dust testifies.

Closeup of a charcoal chinchilla.

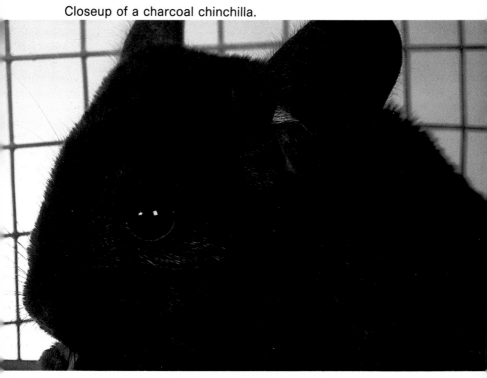

health problems, and even fatalities are possible when it is fed too soon.

Hay for chinchillas must not only be dried on the ground, but it must remain on outside stacks for drying for a week. Hay treated in this manner has the advantage of being dried not only by the sun but also through internal ventilation. This double process inhibits the development of fungus, which can cause a potentially serious health problem. Fungus causes acute diarrhea, which can lead to chronic digestive tract diseases, especially in young animals when left untreated for too long.

Some chinchilla breeders also feed timothy hay, oat straw, or oat hay (oats cut while still in flower or shortly thereafter and then dried). It must be stated here that there is nothing wrong with this type of food. However, caution must be exercised since farmers rarely put much effort into drying these types of hay and straw, which then may possibly give rise to the danger of fungus development.

It is really not necessary to go to great extremes to obtain a particular type of hay. Hay from plains or lowlands is just as useful as hay cut in alpine regions. Yet it is important that it be from the season's first mowing and from a lean type of soil. When harvesting hay it is important that it does not rain.

Hay given as chinchilla food must always be dry (brittle) enough to crush in the hand. During autumn and spring most chin breeders have some difficulties with keeping hay dry. The humidity is very high during those periods, and hay absorbs humidity, loses its crispness, and becomes tough. Feeding hay of such inferior quality usually leads to diarrhea. When this occurs most breeders will attempt to treat this problem with a constipating agent. This is totally wrong. When diarrhea occurs, that is, when a number of animals are coming down with it at the same time, I would immediately direct my attention to the hay and start drying it again.

Hay can be dried in a basket on top of a stove, making sure the basket and hay are lifted above the stove so they cannot catch fire. Many breeders dry their hay by placing it for one or two days in a cardboard box next to a radiator. Some just spread it out on the lawn where it can be re-dried in the sun. If this method is used, make sure animals such as cats, dogs, chickens, mice, and various pests do not walk in it. Hay contaminated with urine and feces can cause diseases and mortalities among chinchillas.

Many breeders feed hay twice a day, in the morning and again in the evening. I maintain that this is quite correct, yet it must not be done in excess. When there is too much hay the animals will pull more out of the hopper than they can eat. Consequently there is the risk that the animals will compact the hay on the cage floor, possibly soil it, and then feed on it again, leading to fungus problems.

Thistles, which are prevalent in alpine hay, are difficult to handle for the breeder, yet they are delicacies for chinchillas. Breeders who use alpine hay must pay special attention to weed out such poisonous and potentially lethal plants such as belladonna, ferns, and meadow saffron. Even in a dried condition these plants are easy to recognize. The breeder is cautioned against using forest hay, which comes from forest clearings where poisonous plants are more common.

Instead of hay, chinchillas can occasionally be given hay cubes, which are commonly used for farm animals. These cubes are pelleted chopped hay held together by an inert binding agent. Hay is known as roughage and is required by the intestinal flora of chinchillas. It also promotes proper digestion. When pellets are being fed on top of even more pellets this does have detrimental effects. Most chinchilla breeders who have tried in this

Upper photo: Portrait of a chinchilla family group: the youngsters shown here with their parents are all less than two months old. *Lower photo:* Beige female shown with a brown velvet male and a silver male.

The intelligence and keen curiosity of the chinchilla are immediately evident in this closeup.

manner to circumvent the often difficult acquisition of hay and the associated storage problems have inevitably returned to the customary feeding of hay within a short period of time.

CHEWING

Chinchillas are rodents, and their front teeth (incisors) grow continuously. In order to avoid dental problems they must be given ample opportunity to grind down their front teeth. For that reason chinchillas are commonly given natural pumice stones or short branches from hazelnut trees. Branches from apple trees are also suitable, but care has to be taken that they do not come from trees that have been sprayed with insecticides.

GREEN FOOD

The topic of green food is often hotly debated among chinchilla breeders. Personally, I am against using green food, with one exception—treating "fur biting." Again, I am basing my conviction on farm animal husbandry practices. To support my view I refer to cows that are kept exclusively indoors in stalls where they are fed only dry food—these animals appear to be least susceptible to diseases.

Offering green food means essentially nothing more than a change of diet. Chinchilla breeders who have given green food to their animals will have noticed digestive disturbances in the form of loose feces and diarrhea. This invariably causes concern, and the breeder starts to experiment: first he treats the diarrhea, and then he treats the resultant constipation. Finally, the digestive system of such an animal has become so disturbed that it may take months until it has recovered. This, of course, has negative effects on the entire metabolism of an animal, which in turn has a detrimental effect on the animal's reproduction.

There are many examples of this. Although I always warn novices against using green food, I can not help but notice that my well-meaning advice sometimes goes unheeded. One chinchilla breeder gave "selected" green foods, such as dandelion and lettuce leaves, to her animals. The outcome of this was that one animal suddenly refused the normal diet of hay, pellets, and mixed food. The feces became thin, elongated, and slimy. The animal lost weight and its fur took on a rough, untidy appearance. Having tried various remedies in vain, this woman finally came to see me to ask for my advice. When I questioned her I found out about the green food diet, the consequences, and her attempts to cure it with home remedies. I took the sick animal from her, placed it in a separate cage, and offered it at first only water with Karlsbad salt. After two days the animal (it was a female) slowly began to feed, and from then on it recovered rapidly from day to day. A few weeks later the original owner came by and was indeed surprised that this animal was still alive.

The reasons for my negative views on green food are essentially based on my own costly experiences with this type of diet. I am aware that some chinchilla breeders swear by green food, but I tend to advise beginners strongly against it.

Closeup of the genital area of an adult female chinchilla. The vaginal opening appears as a mere slit and runs transversely, situated midway between the anus and the urethral cone.

Facing page:
The upper photo shows the genital area of a fully mature male chinchilla, and the lower photo shows a closeup of the genital area of a younger (but still adult) male. Notice that the space between the penis and the anus is much greater than the space between the anus and the urethral cone in the female.

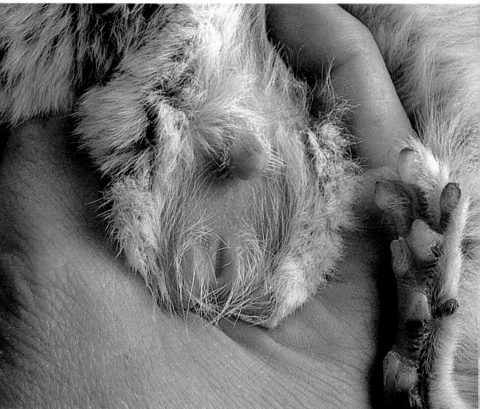

CHANGE OF DIET

There can never be enough warnings against changing the diet of chinchillas, because switching from one diet to another always involves risks. Since diet changes in the past caused considerable damage and expensive losses to breeders, I believe that it is of paramount importance to discuss this topic in some detail.

Unfortunately, chinchilla breeders are only too easily inclined to change the diet of their animals, be it in response to advertising by feed manufacturers or as an (erroneous) economic measure (rabbit pellets!). When the change of diet is instituted and problems begin to arise, one then rarely ever hears anything further about it.

If a change in diet should become necessary it should preferably be done on young animals at an age of about five to eight months. Under no circumstances should the diet of pregnant or nursing females be changed. Only those animals that are given constantly the same diet and same amounts will produce progeny regularly.

ALL-PELLET DIETS

With the increase in my animal stock the work load involved in care and feeding of these animals on a mixed diet increased correspondingly, and I started to think about how I could reduce the work load involved. At meetings with other breeders the feeding of pellets, hay, and water was always described as being completely without danger and totally sufficient, so I started to follow this type of feeding with my chins. At that time I had no previous experience with such a diet, but instead I trusted the allegedly experienced breeders and was persuaded to use the much simpler and easier straight pellet diet.

I have to emphasize that I initiated this dietary change very, very slowly. At first I gradually reduced the amount of my proven mixed food and balanced the daily food rations with pellets. Apart from the fact that the animals did not appear to be thrilled with their caretaker, there initially were no visible signs of any problems. After a few weeks, however, some animals had convulsions that manifested themselves in twitching and trembling over the entire body. The chinchillas laid down on one side as if they were suffering from a loss of equilibrium. When an animal was touched it tried to flee but could not get up and run away. In mild cases such convulsions would last just a few minutes; more serious cases required longer to recover. (When this occurs it is best to leave the animal alone; do not remove it from the cage, because this would upset it even more.)

The cases of convulsions in my animals started to increase, so I started to worry about this situation. First I asked other breeders whether they had observed convulsions following a change of diet. Their answers varied. Most of them indicated that the pellets I was using appeared to be unsuitable. I was advised to try another brand. Who would not have followed such advice?!

So I purchased different pellets and started to feed these to my animals. For starters, all the chinchillas came down with diarrhea. Since the treatment I initiated was obviously less than satisfactory, I turned to my colleagues again for more advice. Their reply was that this reaction was normal and I had nothing to worry about. Beyond that I was also told unequivocally not to give my mixed food in addition to the new pellets, since they already contained all the essential nutritional elements, vitamins, minerals, and trace elements required by the animals. The diarrhea did stop, but it recurred periodically.

When I had the first mortalities due to diarrhea among my subadult animals, I was at a loss. When several pregnant females aborted I finally stopped feeding

Their fur is not the only thing that makes chinchillas beautiful; the entire animal has an attractive appearance.

the straight pellet diet and again started giving mixed food supplements. Now the convulsions ceased, the feces became normal again, and the animals gave an overall impression of good health.

As if this bad experience with a pure pellet diet was not enough, I let myself be persuaded twice more to try a pure pellet diet. Every time I did, I encountered the same serious problems with my animals. During the most recent change of diet some of the various symptoms did not occur and there were no mortalities, so I was nearly inclined to rely solely on a pure pellet diet. The first litters appeared, and then—horror—none of the females was lactating. Since all of them were young females with their first litter, I was convinced that this lack of milk was due to the young age of the females and not the pellet diet. An attempt to feed the young (from the third day on; before that the weak condition of the newborn had gone unnoticed) on a mixture of powdered milk for babies and water failed, although this had worked in other artificial feeding attempts (litters of four) before. Finally, when established females were also unable to nurse their newborn litters, it became clear to me that the problem lay solely with the pure pellet diet (without mixed food supplement). It took 27 mortalities before I realized the cause of these deaths.

I changed the diet—immediately and for good—back to my proven feed regimen: pellets, mixed food, hay, and water. No other breeder will ever be able to convince me again that a diet of pellets, hay, and water is sufficient for chinchillas. Without the supplement of mixed food there simply can be no decisive and long-lasting breeding success with these animals.

Nowadays many breeders hold a different opinion than I do, and it is common to find a sole diet of only pellets, hay, and water being successfully fed. Pelleted food has indeed been constantly improved nutritionally, and the vitamin levels have been increased. It is, however, important that only fresh pellets are fed, and they must not be older than six weeks from the date of manufacture, since the vitamins have a limited shelf-life. A daily ration of 20 g per animal is considered sufficient. Personally, though, I will stick with my mixed diet. It may take more time to produce and feed, but it has never caused me problems.

DRINKING WATER

Years ago chinchilla breeders believed that chinchillas could go without drinking water. Since then experience has shown that this incorrect. Chinchillas receive dry food and so must be given drinking water fit for human consumption. Fresh spring water is the most suitable type, but it is not always easy to get. For us here in the Alps, our excellent alpine water relieves us of this problem.

Chlorinated water from metropolitan water supply systems probably creates more fertility problems than we would like to believe. If this is the only type of water available, it is advisable to boil it and add a pinch of sea salt. To satisfy the water requirements of chinchillas with substantial fruit supplements (apples) may be worth while trying. If anything, this would certainly reduce their water demand.

Remember that it is very important that the water bottles be replenished daily. The chins must receive fresh water with their evening food. Unused water must be discarded at each feeding. Each filling of the water bottles must be preceded by a thorough rinsing, and twice a week the bottles should be thoroughly cleaned to remove any algae growth. The best way to achieve proper cleaning is by using mild dish washing detergents followed by a thorough rinsing with clean water. Algae growth on the sides of the water bottles *must* be

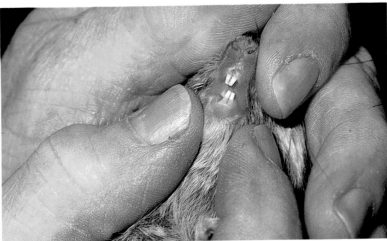

Upper photo: A small three-sided file is being used to file the teeth of an adult male. *Lower photo:* Closeup of the mouth of a one-day-old baby chinchilla, exhibiting incisors that have not yet attained their eventual yellow coloration.

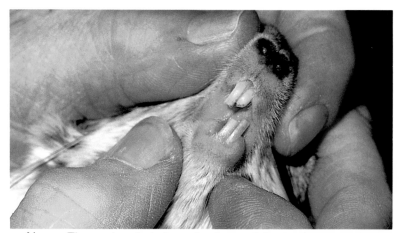

Above: The maloccluded teeth of an adult chinchilla, showing slanting incisors. *Below:* The correct yellow-to-orange color of an adult chinchilla's incisors is evident here.

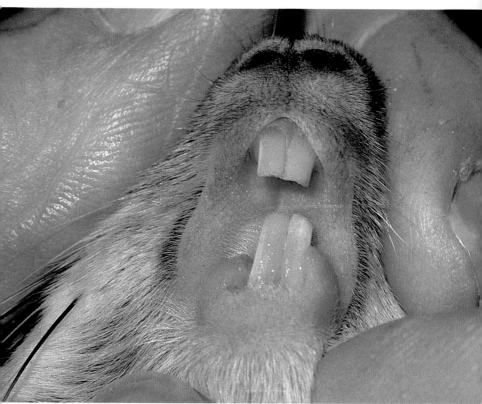

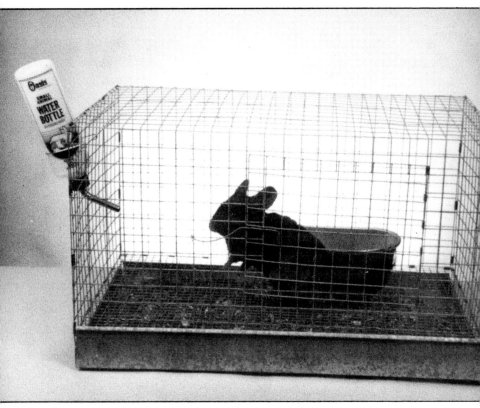

The water bottle on this cage is correctly situated in such a way that the cage inhabitant can sip easily from it; the orifice of the bottle should be readily available to the drinking chinchilla.

removed. The bottle stoppers must also be cleaned and chewed drip tubes replaced regularly.

It can not be emphasized enough that cleanliness is of paramount importance. Any carelessness while cleaning the drinking bottles can easily lead to diseases and mortalities. Suggestions to use open drinking containers such as bowls, dishes, and cups must be categorically rejected. Animals, like humans, like to drink clear, fresh water from clean containers!

4. The Dust Bath

One of the most important aspects of chinchilla keeping is for these animals to be able to bathe in a suitable sand or dust. This serves as a cleansing medium, removes excess natural oils from the fur, promotes the well-being of the animals. A dust bath must be offered daily, preferably before the morning feeding. After all, chinchillas are typical nocturnal animals and most of their activities (playing, running around, mating, fighting) take place at night, so in the morning the animals are "sweaty," the fur is matted, and skin respiration is inhibited. The dust bath in the morning cleans up and loosens the fur again. It should not exceed 10 to 15 minutes for each animal, however.

The dust becomes slightly soiled with urine at each bath. This must be corrected immediately, since it tends to stain the fur. Droppings may be removed about once a week by sifting the dust.

Chinchilla breeders use different kinds of dust or sand and bath tubs. It is left up to the individual to determine what works best for his animals. If fine-grained clean quartz sand is used, talcum powder should be added. Special chinchilla dust is now available in some pet shops.

The dust baths as such and the dust in particular must be given much attention. Experience has shown that those breeders who 'skimp' with the bath sand or

Baby chinchillas being supported in the palm of their owner's hand; as cute as adult chinchillas are, babies are even cuter.

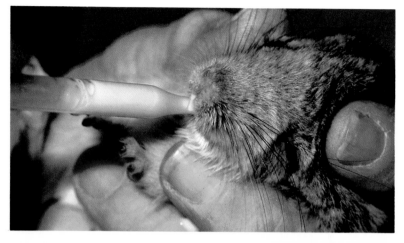

Upper photo: Hand-feeding a baby chinchilla from an eye dropper holding warm milk. *Lower photo:* Fourteen-day-old twins nursing from their mother. The curled tail of the baby chin at right in the photo is a sign of contentment and good health.

even who service 20 or more animals with only a single bath produce ragged-looking chins even when they own top-quality stock.

Each animal must have its own dust bath. This avoids the transmission of parasites and infectious diseases. Frequent cleaning of the dust prevents its complete replacement; it only needs to be "topped up" occasionally. Coarse quartz sand, river sand, construction (brick layer's) sand, or sand from open sand pits must NOT be used. Only very fine sands and dusts are suitable; in nature chinchillas bathe in powdered volcanic ash.

Although chinchillas are very clean animals, they can be turned into real pigs by thoughtless actions of the breeder. Chins that have not had a dust bath for weeks or even months get used to not having it and later can not be persuaded to use a dust bath again. Also, young chinchillas that do not become familiar with a dust bath while still being nursed will refuse to use the bath once they are weaned.

5. Breeding Room Cleanliness

Chinchillas are animals that like and appreciate cleanliness. Therefore, it is absolutely imperative that the breeder maintains his facilities, including cages and equipment, in impeccable condition at all times.

DAILY CLEANING

Certain daily cleaning chores are absolutely essential. Leftover scattered food remnants and hay must be removed prior to any feeding. You can see yourself how important this is when your animals feed on these leftovers and then get diarrhea. If the cage is cleaned up daily this sort of problem does not occur.

The food containers must also be cleaned out and leftovers must be thrown away. It is absolute nonsense to "recycle" pellets that have fallen through onto the bottom tray and feed them to the animals again. Chinchilla "breeders" who do this should give up breeding if they can not afford fresh food for their animals!

Once the daily cleaning chores have been completed and the morning food has been given, the breeding room must be swept out. The daily cage cleaning must become a regular routine that should be done at or about the same time every day, either in the morning or evening. It should be done preferably during the feed-

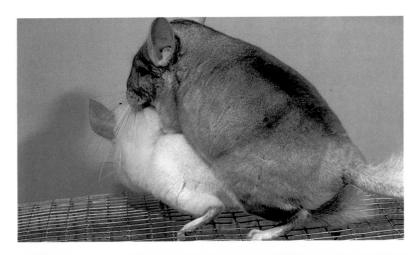

Upper photo: A beige male mating with a pink/white female.
Lower photo: The baby chinchilla shown here is truly brand-new—just two minutes old!

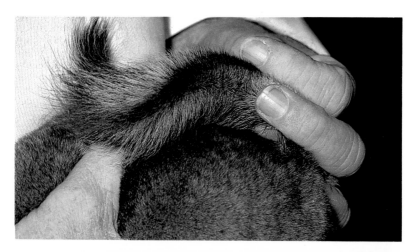

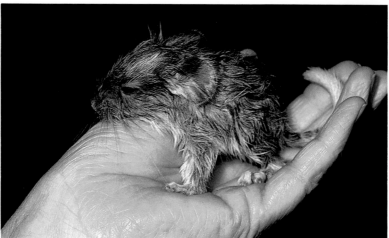

Upper photo: Note the contrast between the fine-textured fur on the chinchilla's body and the much coarser hair on the tail. *Lower photo:* A one-hour-old baby chinchilla with its eyes completely open and appearing a good deal less bedraggled than the two-minute-old baby shown on the facing page.

ing time, because then it causes the least stress to the animals.

WEEKLY CLEANING

The cage tray must be emptied once a week and re-filled with fresh bedding. Loose fur, which tends to stick to the sides and partitions and become regular dust collectors, must be removed. Similarly, the dust baths must be cleaned out and the dust replaced.

During either the weekly cleaning or once a month, the wire of the cage bottom should be cleaned by lightly going over it with a blowtorch and then wiping it clean with a cloth.

MAJOR CLEANING

There must be a major, very thorough cleaning of the entire facility about twice a year—once in spring (May) and another one in fall (September). The former is needed to clean up after the long winter months, while the latter serves as preparation for the coming winter.

Many breeders use a mild disinfectant for cleaning cages, in which case it goes without saying that this must be followed by a thorough rinsing with water. I personally have had good experiences with caustic soda. This general cleaning is also the appropriate time for any repairs, change-over of cages, etc.

Disturbances to the animals must be kept to a minimum during all cleaning activities, and care must be taken not to stress pregnant or nursing females.

6. Diseases and First Aid

With correct care and maintenance, chinchillas are very resistant to diseases and not as susceptible as many other animals. It has been my experience that the most common disease problems are constipation, diarrhea, and fungus infection. The treatment of all of these is quite possible without any special medication.

CONSTIPATION

Constipation is most commonly caused by change in location (breed shows, etc.), change of facility, change in diet, too much mixed food and, of course, the use of green food, which I have already strongly discouraged. It is imperative that everyone (especially the beginner) who sets up a breeding colony of chinchillas gives each newly acquired animal on the very first day a pinch (tip of a knife blade) of Karlsbad salt mixed in sufficient drinking water to fill half a bottle. It is important that each animal is actually seen drinking this entire volume. An examination of the droppings the next morning will tell whether a repeat treatment is necessary or not.

In a case of constipation due to too much mixed food, the animal is picked up and given a somewhat stronger Karlsbad salt solution administered directly into the mouth. This must be done at least three times a day. The effect of this treatment can also be seen in the droppings that night or, at the latest, next morning. If these

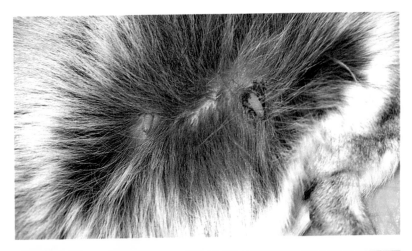

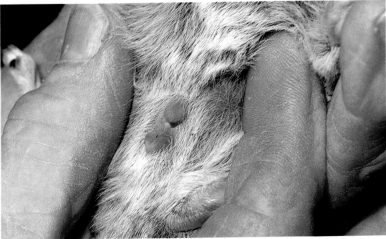

Upper photo: Closeup of the nipples of a nursing female chinchilla. *Lower photo:* The genital area of a one-day-old chinchilla; even at that very young stage of its life the animal can be seen to be a male because of the space between anus and penis.

Upper photo: Two-week-old babies safely nestled in their owner's hands. Special care must be exercised when handling baby chinchillas, as the treatment they receive when very young can affect their socialization in later life. *Lower photo:* The mosaic female shown here is exactly 53 days old and completely trusting of its owner.

recommended measures are not complied with it can lead to intestinal prolapse or even an intestinal occlusion. Even a veterinarian then could no longer save the animal.

Some breeders use paraffin (kerosine), which is given orally and as an enema. This is not required when the above procedures have been initiated. Breeders are strongly advised AGAINST using castor oil. It is of the greatest importance that all breeders (experts and novices alike) consistently monitor the droppings of their animals. For a thorough check the tray must be emptied and the bedding (sawdust) replaced.

REMEMBER THE FOLLOWING BASIC RULE: IF THE ANIMAL IS NOT FEEDING PROPERLY, CHECK ITS DROPPINGS!

If a female in advanced pregnancy gets constipated shortly before giving birth, the Karlsbad salt solution can also be used, in this case quite effectively. It is alleged that some breeders have even given enemas to such animals, with a rather predictable outcome! One breeder was worried and checked the droppings of his animals twice a day. He noticed that one female had smaller droppings than the rest. Although it is a fact that droppings are highly variable in size among different animals, he could not be dissuaded from the idea that this female had constipation. He then proceeded to administer a castor oil enema via a catheter, and the animal immediately aborted. After that it was immediately given a dust bath that was not particularly clean. This led to a tumor-like swelling on the vagina, and the animal finally died. I can not caution enough AGAINST using castor oil enemas.

An excellent prophylactic against constipation in females (which tend to eat the afterbirth and so expose their intestinal tract to an unaccustomed type of food) is once again Karlsbad salt given in drinking water. This promotes digestion of the unaccustomed food and also effects its proper excretion.

DIARRHEA

We distinguish two types of diarrhea: 1) diarrhea in juveniles due to *overfeeding*, and 2) diarrhea in older animals due to *improper food* and/or incorrect feeding.

Juveniles tend to overfeed, which inevitably results in diarrhea. In order to prevent this from becoming a chronic condition the food ration must be returned to normal as an immediate prophylactic measure. In addition, Terramycin powder must be given with the drinking water. Food must NOT be withheld.

Older animals often get diarrhea from having eaten contaminated or spoiled food or damp hay. Here too a change in the droppings is indicative of a dirty cage. The breeder must immediately investigate which food is causing the problem. Once this has been detected, immediate withdrawal of it corrects the problem. If, however, the diarrhea continues, all feeding must cease immediately for a day and Terramycin must be added to the drinking water. Then normal feeding is resumed. Terramycin is known to cure even the most stubborn cases of diarrhea.

It is important not to lose patience if the droppings do not immediately return to a firm consistency. However, the diarrhea condition is critical when the droppings have become nearly fluid and give off a foul smell. This too can be treated with Terramycin, as indicated above. Some breeders administer a laxative (castor oil) in cases like this so that the digestive tract is emptied out and healing can take place more rapidly. This is contraindicated by the opinion of my veterinarian. He believes that castor oil if used on such small animals is actually damaging to the digestive tract. In other words,

An 18-day-old female black velvet female in very good condition.

Closeup of the genital area of a week-old female chinchilla.

A chinchilla baby with his porcelain rodent friend. *Below:* Closeup of a front paw of a young chinchilla; note the absence of claws.

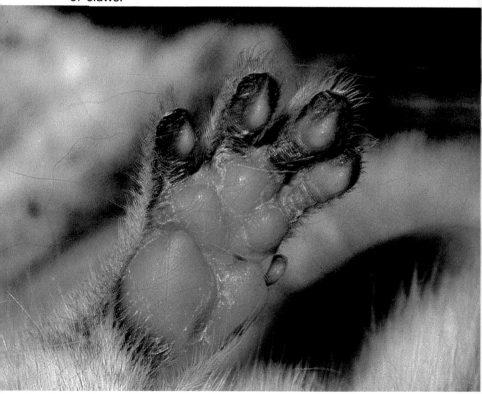

the castor oil antagonizes the already affected intestine even further. Therefore, it is better to use paraffin oil (kerosine), since this is inert to the digestive tract. In any event, Karlsbad salt when given in drinking water always has a healing effect. It facilitates cleaning and emptying of the affected intestine in the case of diarrhea as well as constipation. It also reactivates the intestinal flora.

There is little cause for concern when soft but still normally shaped droppings occur occasionally in bucks just before copulation and in females shortly after having given birth.

HAIR RINGS IN BUCKS

After repeated copulations, a ring of hairs may form around the penis in bucks, and the animals can not remove it themselves. This condition is often overlooked by novice breeders. If it is not corrected the organ will atrophy and the animal dies a painful death. The external symptom is obvious: the buck sits lethargically around in his run and takes in very little food because he is in pain. This then requires immediate help.

The buck must be taken out of the cage and closely examined. If the presence of a hair ring is noticed it must slowly be dissolved in lukewarm water and then cautiously removed by hand. Special care must be taken not to injure the penis with finger nails. Usually the relevant muscles are already weakened to such an extent that the animal can no longer move the penis. After removal of the hair some petroleum jelly should be cautiously applied to the penis and it must be gently pushed back into its skin. Afterward the animal should be closely monitored to see if it has regained full use of the penis.

KARLSBAD SALT AND POISONING

Karlsbad salt has been mentioned repeatedly in previous chapters as a prophylactic and cure for constipation as well as diarrhea. It also has been shown to be an effective remedy against poisonings. Karlsbad salt is often kept in solution, and it is important that the bottle is vigorously shaken before the salt is dispensed. The salt is a rather simple mixture of potassium sulfate, sodium sulfate, sodium chloride, and sodium bicarbonate, but it definitely is as effective in its way as any modern "wonder drug." Do not confuse it with Epsom salts, which contains mostly magnesium sulfate.

Poisonings can occur from the consumption of spoiled or poisonous substances. The latter are sometimes found in hay, such as cock's foot, ferns, and meadow saffron, and also in spoiled pellets (fungus) or in mixed food. Seed grains are often treated with poisonous substances (mercuric nitrate, lead) in order to render them unfit for human and animal consumption—such treated seed grains of course should never be brought near chinchilla facilities. Poisonous ingredients in ointments and other home remedies used by breeders to treat swellings or other injuries can also cause poisoning when taken internally.

It is imperative that poisoning symptoms be recognized early. They often manifest themselves in paralysis, best seen during feeding. The animal is no longer capable of swallowing the food; breathing becomes labored since the function of the respiratory tract has become impaired; and the eyes lose their dark color and become marbled with white.

Animals with these symptoms must be given a strong solution of Karlsbad salt in a concentration of one part salt and five parts water. This solution is given three times a day to the animal. Shortly thereafter the para-

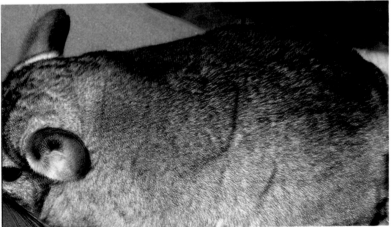

Upper photo: Male and female day-old baby chinchillas, the male showing definite space between anus and genitals. *Lower photo:* The "priming lines" on a standard chinchilla show up as dark lines on the fur.

Upper photo: Triplets—two pink/white males and a mosaic female. *Lower photo:* A one-hour-old baby chinchilla and its parents, the mother more completely visible.

lytic symptoms will regress and the animal starts feeding again. After eight days the animal will have regained its normal health. It is important, of course, that the animal was in good physical condition when the problem was detected and that treatment was begun without delay.

FUNGUS INFECTIONS

In my experience a fungus infection is almost invariably the result of a mechanical injury that subsequently becomes infected and which then gives rise to the formation of a sort of scabies. Such fungus infections in chinchillas can be cured easily. The affected areas are dusted with a veterinary fungicide. Check with your veterinarian to see which one he recommends. One teaspoon is also added to the dust bath, where it must be mixed in well. I usually add the fungicide routinely once a month to the dust bath of each animal as a prophylactic. Since I have instituted these regular preventive treatments fungus infections have not occurred in my facility. I have also noticed that fungus infections in chinchillas are more prevalent during hot, humid periods of the year.

Another cause of fungus infections is fungus spores contained in hay. When this hay becomes damp during prolonged rainy periods in summer or fall, the spores tend to develop unless the hay is sufficiently dried again before feeding and the dust bath contains a fungicidal additive.

If a fungus infection occurs in one animal, the entire breeding group must be treated because the incubation period (time from initial infection with the fungus until the disease breaks out) may be up to three weeks. Actually, since fungus infections are so variable and are sometimes very difficult to treat, it is best to always check with your veterinarian before starting any massive dosing of an entire facility.

It is important, of course, that fungus infections are detected early. They are more easily seen around the snout or eyes. The fur begins to thin out and hair falls out; the skin underneath is usually reddish. If the fungus is resistant to chemicals and already widespread, especially in the anal and genital regions, consult your veterinarian.

DISINFECTION

If an animal dies of a disease or of unknown causes, its cage must be properly disinfected BEFORE another animal is placed in it. The procedure to follow is to immediately remove the cage from the breeding room and take it outside to thoroughly wash it with a disinfectant. Afterward the cage must be properly rinsed, preferably using a garden hose and plenty of water. Then this cage must be permitted to dry in the sun for a few days before it is used again for other animals.

INDUCING WEIGHT LOSS

First a practical example: Some years ago a chinchilla breeder took to a fur industry teaching seminar a buck that had good colors but would not mate. When the animal was skinned there were large fatty deposits along its neck, front and hind thighs, and around the genitals. The poor animal was simply too fat to mate, not just uninterested. When asked why the animal had been overfed the answer was, "Because the animal enjoyed the food!"

Chinchilla pelts do not mature properly when the animals are too fat. Fat deposits cause sparse hair growth and prevent the development of good fur density. Unfortunately, breeding animals—males as well as fe-

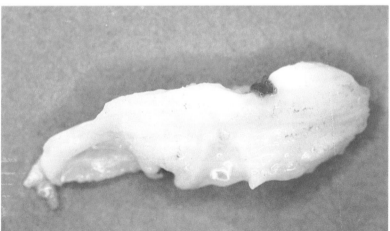

Upper photo: A standard gray male showing poor color and poor-quality fur. *Lower photo:* This is a fresh white vaginal plug from a mated female.

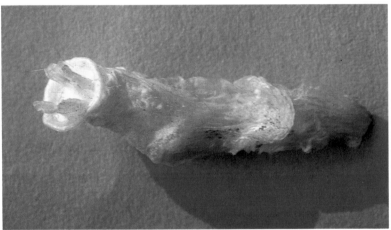

Upper photo: Genital area of adult female, with anus and papilla almost touching and closed vagina between; this female is not in estrus. *Lower photo:* Typically dried out and yellowed vaginal plug found several days after a mating.

The diet of chinchillas has a definite effect on their willingness and ability to produce young. Poorly fed (meaning, essentially, too richly fed) males become less aggressive in pursuing females, and females conceive less readily and also have problems in nursing their young.

males—are often given too much pelleted food and in addition they even get "munchies" (raisins!). The consequences of such systematic fattening diets are:

a) the bucks tend to become lethargic and do not mate;

b) females have difficulty conceiving, and when they become pregnant and give birth they suffer from a lack of milk.

An alarming sign that chinchillas are being overfed is when the food bowl is not empty at the next feeding! Food rations should be such that all food is eaten by the time the next feeding comes around. The animals must be really hungry at their regularly scheduled feeding times and virtually hang at the wire when the breeder enters the room. When the extreme opposite occurs— no desire to feed at all—then something is wrong; usually the animal is constipated!

Now to the "slimming diet," which can be simply stated as "E. H.!" = eat half! A fat animal is given only a small maintenance ration—the pellet ration is reduced by half. If the animal also gets mixed food in the morning, this must be omitted for a week and replaced by an apple wedge only. Water is given only once a day. After one week the normal diet is restored, though of course NOT to such an extent as before when the "slimming diet" had to be instituted.

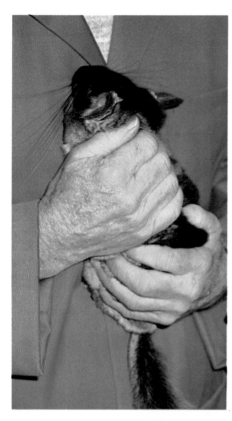

Left:
An acceptable method
of holding a pet
chinchilla is to cradle it
snugly against the
chest, securely
supported. *Below:* A
standard-colored
black-eyed chinchilla.

Closeup of a brown velvet male accepting a treat from its owner's fingers.

7. Fur Biting

In my 20 years of experience as a chinchilla breeder I have yet to meet a breeder who has not encountered the problem of fur biting. I am also skeptical of claims by chinchilla food manufacturers that using their particular food pellets will solve the fur biting problem. Here I can not help but observe that this sort of advertising may well increase their cash flow but does little for the breeders except give them false hopes. So far there is simply no universal cure for fur biting. Breeders must still rely on individual treatments based upon an investigation to find the cause of each case. Only those breeders who know the causes—and there are many causes—are able to deal with this problem reasonably well. Although my discussions on this topic may not guarantee a decisive victory, I am of the opinion that by adhering to some specific countermeasures the breeder will be spared much aggravation if he initiates preventive measures in time.

The experienced breeder easily recognizes the first signs of fur biting, but for the benefit of beginners let me briefly explain them. It may seem improbable, but there are still breeders around who are not able to spot fur biting after they have had their animals for more than 12 months. These people may even believe that

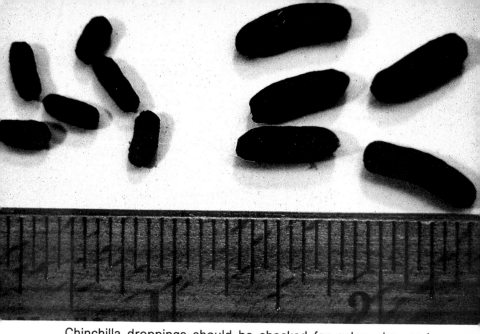

Chinchilla droppings should be checked for color, size, and texture; the droppings shown here are referenced next to a ruler scaled in inches to show comparative size. The group of droppings at the right is from a different animal from those shown on the left.

their animals are undergoing some type of maturing process and are getting a dark pelt. To novices this may indeed appear to be the case, but how are they to know otherwise? Fur biting in chinchillas has a variety of causes, all of which are attributable to incorrect maintenance. They are essentially mistakes made by inexperienced—as well as occasionally by experienced—breeders in their animal husbandry methods.

Causes include improper accommodation of breeding stock; damp or drafty breeding rooms; storage rooms with inadequate ventilation; overcrowing of the breeding facility; incorrect diet and nutrition (without hay or with just pressed hay cubes); irregular feedings in respect to type of food and feeding times; and just plain careless maintenance. A further cause may be noise pollution—proximity to crowded streets, airports, visits by

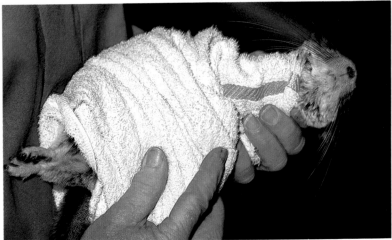

Upper photo: This brown velvet baby shows the ruby eye color seen on some chinchillas. *Lower photo:* This chinchilla has been fully wrapped in a towel for handling and examination, with front legs securely held and rear legs extended.

This pair consists of a beige female and a brown velvet male.

relatives. Dogs and cats must never be permitted into the breeding room! All these factors tend to upset chinchillas, and if not eliminated they will have detrimental effects on the animals. At first the animals become nervous, then they go virtually crazy and start to chew on their fur. All animals, whether old or young, can get involved in this sort of activity.

Many of the causes listed collectively under maintenance mistakes can be avoided when the chinchillas are kept as recommended in this book. Some more specific causes and their respective corrective measures are discussed below.

In older females fur biting occurs during pregnancy; in younger breeding females it usually occurs when another young female is added to a polygamous breeding group and the buck is prevented from access during estrus, be it as an oversight or for other reasons. Sometimes a female will chew on her partner if he is incapable of mating or—more commonly—when a new buck is placed together with an old female. There can also be fur biting because of suppressed sex drive in males that are not used for breeding. Sometimes the first signs of fur biting can be seen in young animals that are still with their mother. They gnaw at each other's fur or that of their mother. Here it is usually a case of food envy, which can be eliminated by increasing the food rations.

Initially such gnawing causes dark patches on the back or along the flanks of the pelt. These get larger and larger so that these areas eventually become rather unsightly. If such a gnawed-on animal is taken out of the cage and you blow gently against one of these areas, you can see how the fur has been gnawed down in what looks like little steps. When such changes are seen in the pelts of chinchillas—whether old or young animals—there is no doubt that they have been caused by fur biting.

Older breeding females that chew on their own fur during late pregnancy or after having given birth are believed to be suffering from hormonal deficiencies according to prevailing veterinary opinion. Moreover, experience has shown that up to 50% of the progeny of such females also become fur biters! My observations in this particular area have shown that these females actually were too old for breeding (older than eight years) or that they were progeny of old breeding females. Therefore, it is safe to say that the progeny from breeding stock that is too old will sooner or later become fur biters. I was able to show this experimentally. I placed an eight-year-old buck into a polygamous group consisting of females one to six years old. The result was that the old females produced up to 100% fur-biters and the young females up to 50%.

Since science has so far been unable to come up with an effective remedy against old age and its consequences (in our case, fur biting), the only thing for a chinchilla breeder to do is to remove all old breeding animals when they or their progeny start to gnaw on their fur.

If fur biting occurs suddenly in both young and old females, that were not derived from fur biting parentage, it is probably due to husbandry errors that, when corrected, will eliminate the fur biting problem.

Nutritional deficiencies are today hardly ever reason for fur biting. If losses of this or a similar nature ever occur due to dietary deficiencies, the underlying reason is invariably a spoiled food supply due to incorrect storage or simply food not suitable for chinchillas. One of the main factors in chinchilla nutrition continues to be the quality of the hay. Please reread the section on the importance and problems of hay. If ample hay is fed, this tends to remedy fur biting and keeps fur biting at bay in healthy animals.

I have had also some success in curing fur biters by

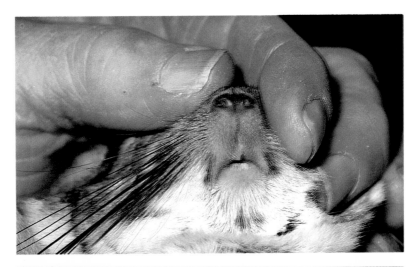

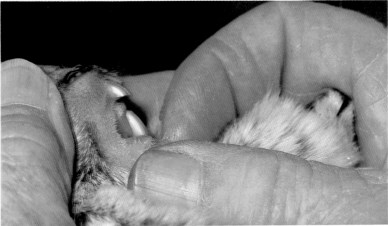

Upper photo: The nose of this chinchilla is clean and dry—a good sign. *Lower photo:* Side view of the incisors of an adult chinchilla, showing good shape.

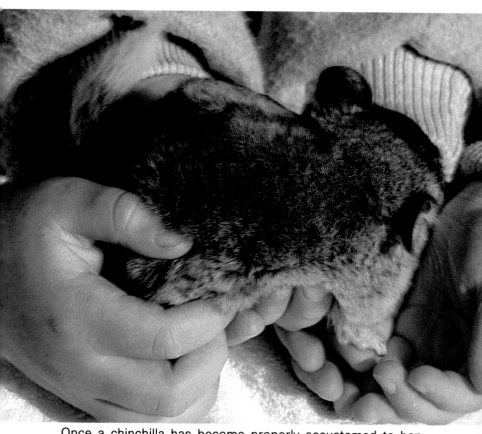

Once a chinchilla has become properly accustomed to handling and has lost whatever fear it might have had of being handled, it snuggles right down and enjoys itself when correctly picked up.

changing their surroundings, such as change of enclosures, as well as with solar radiation (sunshine). However, with the latter special care has to be taken that the animals are exposed to direct sunlight only for a short period of time; one should start with about five minutes and gradually increase this to 20 minutes. Furthermore, chinchillas must get periodic vitamin supplements, either as liquids and powders or, during the summer, green food, dandelions, hazelnut leaves, or nettles.

Prior to any treatment attempts I pull the hairs out of the affected areas so that I can monitor whether gnawing has stopped or not.

8. Mating Chinchillas

WHAT ANIMALS TO START OUT WITH

One of the most frequent questions I am asked is: What quality animals should be used to start up a chinchilla breeding group? This is indeed quite a valid question that can easily be answered. The prime consideration is, of course, the financial resources available. From a breeder's point of view it can be stated quite categorically that one must always start out with the highest quality of breeding animals affordable and *never* with inferior ones.

This raises the question of just what is a good quality animal and what is an inferior one. In answering this question I must equate quality animals with fur quality—what is acceptable and desirable to the fur industry. The pet chinchilla field is too recent to have well-established quality standards. There is no real point (in my opinion) in starting out with breeding stock that produces progeny essentially useless to the industry, although owners of pet stock may be satisfied with merely friendly animals in good health and attractive in appearance. Since my experience is with raising animals for fur, that is the background that I must use to judge chinchilla quality.

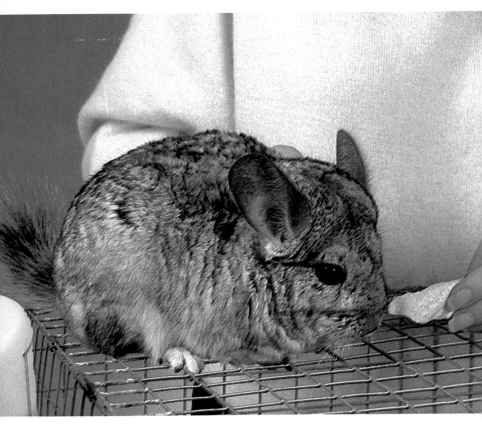

This chinchilla doesn't appear to be overly tempted by the piece of lettuce being offered to it.

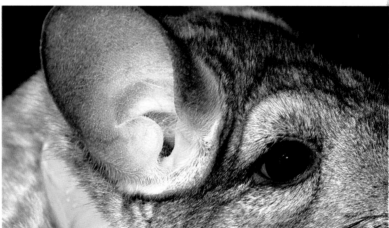

Upper photo: A chinchilla that is being held on the hand should have its hind legs firmly supported. *Lower photo:* The eye and ear of this gray chinchilla both exhibit good shape.

It is incorrect for a beginner to believe that he absolutely must start out with the most expensive, highest quality material. If he has indeed sufficient funds for that I would not discourage him, but this does NOT protect him against losses. The term "highest quality" animals refers to those that are the end product of a selective linebreeding process. Looking after such animals requires considerable experience in chinchilla care and maintenance; they quickly react adversely to any husbandry mistakes. I have seen many novice breeders come to grief with such animals. They may have had the financial resources, but they lacked the necessary experience, patience, and perseverance to look after these animals. The best chinchilla breeders are invariably those who build up their stock from a group of mixed quality breeding animals.

Chinchillas are classified according to several evaluating systems. The evaluation of specific characteristics is expressed in A-points, with the highest level being 15 A-points. From among the various evaluating systems in use, the Willard George System (WGS) is most prevalently used in Europe as well as in North America. My recommendation for all beginners is to start out with females from Category (Class) 14A upward and with bucks from 15A upward of medium, dark, and very dark color tones. Experience has shown that the progeny of such parents usually falls into the categories of Good and Very Good in the classifications of breed and fur quality.

I must warn any beginner against starting out with unevaluated breeding stock—no matter how cheap they may be. Such animal must even be rejected if the vendor states that they are progeny of prize-winning stud material. Invariably those who have come to grief by not listening to this advice will then claim that chinchilla breeding is useless and was simply a poor investment. The reason for such failure is rarely ever admitted; after all, who wants to be embarassed?

SEXING CHINCHILLAS

Astute observers quickly recognize that bucks and females can be distinguished from each other externally. The body shape of males is different from that of females. With few exceptions, males are generally somewhat smaller in overall shape, but the head is wider and more massive than in females. Females are generally larger than males, with a more compact appearance, unless they are young females or one of the Costina types.

A superficial examination of the sex characteristics often tends to confuse the layman. The sex organ of the female is superficially similar to that of the male because the female's urethral cone can be mistaken for a penis. For correct sexing it must always be remembered that the penis in sexually mature males is located about 1 to 1.5 cm away from the anal opening, while the female urethral cone (also referred to as a false penis) is located directly at the anus. The female's vagina is usually not visible. It is positioned vertically halfway between the anus and the urethral cone and runs from side to side; it is firmly closed except during estrus. When a female comes into estrus ("in heat") the vagina opens up and is then clearly visible.

The chinchilla female has six nipples or teats located on the abdomen, three along each side. In contrast to rabbits and cats, a chinchilla female does not lay down to nurse her young. Instead, a few hours after they are born the young will rise onto their hind legs to nurse from their mother.

HOW TO SELECT PAIRS

Today chinchillas are usually kept in polygamous breeding groups on fur farms. Monogamous (individual

Upper photo: Genital area of a female that is in full estrus after having delivered a litter. *Lower photo:* The dark area in this closeup of a chinchilla's coat is the underfur of a fur-chewed animal; the light-colored tip has been chewed off.

pairs) breeding is not cost-effective. In a polygamous breeding group one buck is kept together with several females, usually four to six. The group enclosure consists of several individual compartments for the females and a single run (passage) for the buck. He has access to the female compartments via a narrow hole. A neck or breeding collar made of plastic or metal is attached to each female so that it can not leave its compartment. The male feeds in any of the females' cages or compartments. There is also another type of group breeding known as colony breeding. Here one male and several females are kept together in a large enclosure colony. In spite of many attempts colony breeding has never proven to be successful in chinchillas.

There are often different descriptions given of chinchilla matings, to the extent that this may appear rather complicated to the novice. For the purpose of mating, one distinguishes two age groups: *young animals* (just having reached sexual maturity) and *older animals* (previously mated).

Mating young animals that have just reached sexual maturity is much easier than mating older ones that have been mated before and already have had at least one litter. Young animals, males as well as females, should be mated at an age of eight to nine months. They are essentially very playful at that age. Young females that are mated polygamously with a buck of the same age will get along very well within a short period of time. To achieve this the following has to be observed: The male is placed first in one of the cages of the polygamous enclosure. The remaining empty cages are each filled with a young female wearing a breeding collar. The male settles down initially in his cage where food is available. Once he "explores" the other cages containing the young females he will quickly discover where he is welcome. There he will quickly establish himself with-

The whole process of reaction between male and female potential breeders may go very smoothly or very tempestuously, depending upon many different factors, not the least of which are the relative ages of the animals and their states of health.

out a fight as the "master." As soon as it is obvious that the male is permitted to feed in the cage of another female without being chased away, a female is placed into the male's empty cage.

Caution has to be exercised when an older female is added to a polygamous breeding group of younger animals. In this case the male must not be permitted immediate access to this older female. Usually such a young male can not—due to his inexperience—stand up against the more aggressive, older female. This is often the reason why a young buck is frightened and eventually becomes useless for polygamous breeding. Similar dangers can occur for young females when an older, more experienced buck is placed together with them.

When I was still an inexperienced novice I once lost two young females within a 24-hour period when I placed an old buck together with young females. The male was very aggressive and did not respond to the playful nature of the young females. He was determined to mate, and since the females tended to get away from him he finally became extremeley angry and then simply attacked the females and bit them to death. Before he could attack the third and last female in the group I managed to chase the male away and rescue the remaining young female. When I placed this same male together with experienced females they quickly kept him in check and only surrendered to his courtship advances when they were ready to mate.

It is easy to ruin any young buck through inappropriate mating attempts. However, if the above recommended procedures are followed these problems are avoided. But it is also pointless to keep a young buck separate from females, as such bucks become lethargic and are then unwilling to mate later.

Mating older animals is somewhat more difficult. In order to avoid casualties it often works to mislead the excellent sense of smell in these animals by applying a small amount of some exotic aromatic substance such as perfume, eau de cologne, toothpaste, or eucalyptus cold rub onto the nose of the chinchillas. Apparently this causes them to lose their ability of sexual recognition and they then adjust easier to the presence of a new partner.

The procedure for mating within a breeding group of older animals is the same as for young chinchillas. There is no need to worry if some fur starts to fly (literally) during the courtship. It can, however, happen that a female simply will not mate with a particular buck, and then another buck should be tried out. I do not see a need for special mating cages.

DANGERS DURING MATING

Recognizing danger means dealing with it in an effective manner. Certain dangers may arise during mating when the breeder assembles a new breeding group of chinchillas where some of the older females are replaced by young ones. Then it can happen that one or more of the new young females are in estrus and entice the buck to copulate. Yet, since the access opening to the female's cage compartment is still closed, the male instead may attempt to mate with one of the neighboring females that is not in estrus. This female then will fight off the male, often resulting in a fatality. To the breeder such behavior is usually incomprehensible, since the male used to get along with that particular female and even produced progeny with her. Due to ignorance, this is often described—erroneously—as cannibalism.

For a female newly introduced into an established breeding group there is the danger that it may be killed

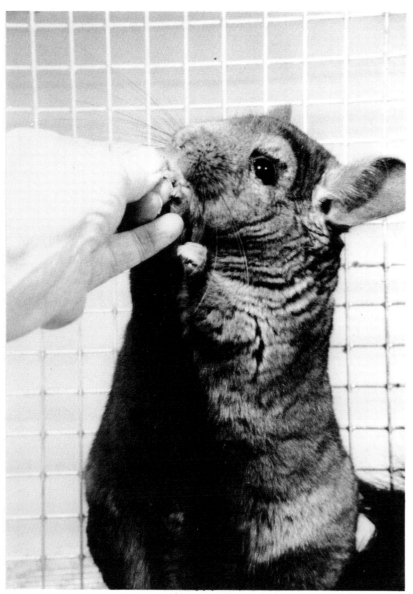

Giving treats to your chinchillas can be fun, because they appreciate them greatly and give good evidence of how much they enjoy them; unfortunately, though, treat-giving can become a destructive practice that fattens, sickens, and eventually kills the chinchillas.

x

101

Full view of an adult male chinchilla. A practiced eye can tell the difference between adult males and females even without recourse to an examination of the animals involved, as the sexes have different body builds.

by the buck. This can also happen if the breeder places yet another female into the empty cage compartment. Moreover, when there are fights between male and some of the females this tends to destabilize and upset the entire group. I believe that chinchilla breeders who do this sort of thing have learned it from rabbit breeders. From an animal husbandry point of view such an undesirable practice has no place in serious chinchilla breeding and must be avoided and rejected.

Breeders are also advised against transferring newly impregnated and pregnant females from their familiar surroundings into another cage. This is often done to get more use out of the male by providing him with additional females for mating. This can have very serious consequences. During very early pregnancy there is the risk of resorption of the fertilized egg. In females during advanced pregnancy this may lead to premature births or stillbirths.

COPULATION

Chinchilla females reach sexual maturity at an age of about five months, but they should not be mated until they are at least eight months old. Sexual maturity manifests itself by the female becoming restless, and a buck will start to "court" her. When such a female is taken out of the cage and closely examined one can see an oval-shaped opening between the anus and the urethral cone. This is the vagina. In young females it can happen that this opening is partially obstructed by a rigid membrane. Applying a suitable skin cream or ointment such as petroleum jelly (or in an emergency even saliva) tends to overcome this problem. Opening of the vagina repeats itself every 28 to 34 days. This does not mean, however, that the female is "in heat," yet the buck will try to copulate then and—after some fighting—he is usually successful.

Depending upon the willingness of a particular female, copulation may occur several times during the night. The next morning one can usually find in the bottom tray the copulatory plug, which is formed by excess sperm ejected from the vagina. Finding this plug is a sure sign that copulation has taken place, but the female may not necessarily conceive. This can only be confirmed after 28 days when the next estrus should occur if the female has not become pregnant. A copulatory plug is rarely found following copulation soon after a litter has been born, since the female will usually eat it. Young as well as older females that have not been fertilized for some time will often excrete an "estrus plug" or "heat plug" with the onset of estrus. This plug is distinctly different from the copulatory plug, being much smaller and almost as wide as long, while copulatory plugs are large, much longer than wide, and are vaguely dumbbell-shaped.

REMOVING THE BUCK

Removing the buck for fear that he would harm the newborn is unfounded, but a "nursery" (especially a nest box) must be available for the young where they can remain when the female mates again. The buck remains with the female while she is giving birth. He works actively as the caring father and helps to dry the young and keep them warm.

In a polygamous breeding colony the buck must be kept from the litter by three days after the litter has been born. This is done by closing off the access hole. Otherwise the young tend to follow the buck along the passage, and when they run into other females they will be mercilessly killed. It is a rare case indeed where the female will not kill the young from another female.

9. Birth

GESTATION

Chinchilla females have a gestation period of 111 days, sometimes plus or minus a few days. It is extremely important that a pregnant chinchilla female is NOT removed from her familiar surroundings! How dangerous this can be, even within the same facility, is best shown by the following example. I read in an American trade journal that large commercial operators removed pregnant females from mating cages and transferred them to nursery cages. Following birth of the litter the female was briefly returned to the mating cage. A similar practice is common among rabbit breeders. This persuaded me to try this method in my own facility.

Although I transferred a particular female only from an upper row of cages to a lower one, it aborted. This was not enough. The two dead young were eaten by the female. I knew from rabbit breeding that females that eat their young after a premature birth become cannibalistic, and I feared that this would happen here. Consequently, I was glad when my anxieties in this respect did not come true. Several months later my chinchilla female got pregnant again and the next litter was quite normal. But I had lost some young and a lot of time, which really meant a loss never to be recovered for any breeder trying to build up his breeding program.

The alert breeder will notice that a female that is about two months into her gestation period tends to feed less than eagerly. This lasts for about one or two days. I am of the opinion that this is due to fetal growth and the physiological burden this places on the female's metabolism. I am convinced that this particular period is decisive as to whether the fetus will be resorbed, die, or continue to develop. For that reason females that have reached the half-way mark in their gestation period must not be sold. Those breeders who closely monitor the weight of pregnant females will discover that after a continuously increasing weight curve, weight increase will suddenly stop at this point and there may even be a weight loss of up to 30 g. When such a female is kept as normal and is not upset or stressed in any way, she suddenly regains her appetite, which manifests itself in an increased food consumption. I believe this supports my contention that chinchillas, especially pregnant females, must be left in peace. This is why I reject weighing the animals. Palpating the pregnant female also is a bad habit that can have detrimental effects if not done correctly.

With young females even the experienced breeder can not always tell whether there is an advanced pregnancy, unless it shows externally in nipple development. I have also frequently observed how breeders, particularly novices, get very excited when they see their pregnant female suddenly lying on her side without any movement. This phenomenon is quite normal and not indicative of anything.

BIRTH

Chinchilla females do not require any help when they

are giving birth to their young. If it happens that complications occur, there is no need for the breeder to panic.

Birth usually occurs during the early morning hours, and the breeder must be prepared for it. If there are no heated nest boxes he must make sure that the room is sufficiently warm. An imminent birth is preceded by labor. The female stretches herself and rears up, emitting mournful sounds. She perspires and obviously suffers pain. During a normal birth this stage lasts only a short period of time, to be followed quickly by the female gently pulling the young out with her teeth, as well as taking care of all other essentials. Should there be twins or even triplets this birth process can last several hours.

When the female eats the afterbirth it is a sure sign that the birth is over. Under no circumstances must the breeder interfere at this point and take the meat-like chunk away from her. A bloodied snout and front paws indicate that the afterbirth has been passed and was eaten.

Sometimes breeders report a lack of milk in a female, but when the animal has been given a correctly balanced diet in regular and sufficient amounts a lack of milk never occurs. In my experience insufficient (or absent) lactation and other deficiencies (convulsions, "goat backs," etc.) are the consequence of incorrect nutrition.

On the day when the female is expected to give birth she must not be given a dust bath. The danger of contracting an inflammation of the womb or vagina is too great. Although there are other opinions on this, I would like to warn the sensible breeder against it. One can hardly expect a dust bath—no matter how clean it is—to be free of bacteria and other disease germs.

PROBLEM BIRTHS

When chinchillas are properly kept and cared for

there are hardly ever any difficulties during the birth. There can be exceptions, of course, just as in any other animal breeding facility. Should there be a problem it is always advisable to consult a veterinarian who has had experience with chinchillas.

Sometimes it can happen that newborn chinchillas are not looked after by their mother, possibly because the entire birth process is not yet over. Consequently the young and still wet newborn is left lying on the bottom wire or among wood shavings and slowly becomes rigid from the cold. At first the breeder may believe he has a dead young, but usually this is not the case. Should this have happened, the almost lifeless newborn is taken out of the cage and an attempt must be made to revive it by slowly warming it up or by applying artificial (mouth-to-mouth) respiration. I have already saved many newborn this way. The best procedure is to take the tiny nearly lifeless creature into your warm hand (forming a fist . . . gently) and then bring it close to your own mouth and breathe easy, short breaths against the mouth of the newborn. It may take up to 15 minutes until the animal responds. Respiration must be maintained until the young chinchilla is able to stand on its own. Under no circumstances must there be direct mouth-to-mouth contact because then the artificial respiration would be too powerful. Once the young has been revived and it is dry, it should be returned to its mother in the cage.

10. Rearing Chins

EARLY FEEDING

Chinchillas are born fully furred and their eyes are fully functional. Within the hour they start to follow their mother and look for her teats for their first meal. It can happen, particularly with large litters, that the young start to fight over access to their mother's teats. Should this happen, the female must be checked for bite injuries on her nipples. If bite marks are seen, then the teeth of the young should be clipped to about half of their length with nail clippers. (You might prefer to have an experienced hand do this for you.) A mild ointment should also be applied to the injured areas on the female.

Supplementary bottle feeding is generally not necessary for litters of up to three young, although this may be advisable when a fourth young is in the litter. The best procedure is to feed just the strongest young with a small doll bottle or pet nursing bottle. A suitable formula consists of one part milk powder or unsweetened condensed milk and two parts lukewarm water (but NOT previously boiled). Spring water is ideal for this purpose; chlorinated tap water must not be used.

Some breeders feed the newborn in "shifts"; in other

words, the young are left individually with the female on a rotational basis. Initially this must be done every two hours for about a week. Thereafter the young can be left with the female continuously.

An important factor is also the size of the food container. From about the eighth day onward the young will attempt to feed from this container, and it is essential that all of them can feed at the same time. This avoids inevitable fighting and potential injuries and damage to the fur. After about six to eight weeks the young are taken away from their mother and are accommodated in individual cages.

FEEDING WEANED YOUNG

This is a point in time when most breeders tend to make the mistake of over-feeding. Ideally the young should receive half an adult ration of pellets at night and half a ration of mixed food in the morning, plus half an adult ration of hay. Only after five or six months can the rations be gradually increased to normal adult rations. During the postweaning period up to an age of about three months is the period when most mortalities occur among the young, simply because they are being overfed.

CAGING

It is absurd for breeders to keep large litters together due to lack of space. After all, these are fur-bearing animals and the fur will not develop the proper quality and the required silkiness within a colony. Even the highest quality animal can hardly produce the best fur under crowded conditions. The conscientious chinchilla breeder will be able to decide four to six months after the young have been placed into individual cages what animals he is going to use for breeding.

ARTIFICIAL REARING

If a female dies shortly after having given birth, the breeder will have to rear the young by artificial means. A doll bottle or pet nursing bottle is the ideal tool for that purpose, using a formula of half condensed milk and half water. If, however, several nursing females are available the motherless young can without any difficulties be given to a "foster mother." The new mother will sniff the young and then usually accept it. The best way is to give the young to a female that gave birth just at about the same time. If the new female rejects the young another female should be tried. Older young cannot be fostered as females will quickly kill the older young of other females.

LITTER SIZE

Healthy, robust chinchilla females generally produce two litters of up to four young per year. This then gives an average of about six to eight young per year per sexually mature female, which is in reality too high. Although there are occasionally litters of five and even six young, usually two or three are stillborn or live only for a short period. Rarely have all of these animals ever been raised by a single female or the breeder.

Litter sizes vary, even those from the same female. One also has to take into consideration that a female sometimes gets sick or does not conceive, so a litter is omitted. Sometimes young do not survive for long. Losses of 5% to 10% are normal at any chinchilla breeding operation. Cases of higher infant mortality are exceptions, and should they occur they are usually the result of husbandry mistakes. Realistically speaking and taking into account all losses, a reproduction rate of three young per year is indeed a good average. We also have to keep in mind that we are dealing with highly inbred animals after decades of selected breeding, so the rate of reproduction is expected to be lower than that of chinchillas in the wild, much as in pedigreed horses and dogs.

Moreover, one also has to consider that litter size and rate of reproduction are largely influenced by environmental conditions (quiet location, animals not unduly disturbed or stressed), nutrition, and ambient temperature. Reduction of the temperature by 10°C has a significantly detrimental effect on the mating willingness of bucks, on litter sizes, and on the newborn young when they are still wet. Much can be said for energy savings, but chinchilla production is not the place for it. On the contrary, lost production may well exceed in value that of any savings effected by reduced energy consumption.

Commercial experiences have shown that the rate of reproduction in a farm holding more than 100 breeding females is lower, with about 2.54 young per female per year. The main reason for this probably lies in the fact that there is no longer so much individual attention, particularly during times of crisis such as complications at birth, given to the specific maintenance and care for the newborn. This can happen even in establishments running only 30 breeding females. Individual care slowly diminishes and details and events in individual cages are overlooked. Losses start to occur at the birth of litters or during the following critical three weeks.

Small breeding establishments of up to 20 breeding females may achieve—with optimum care and attention—an annual average of four young that survive, but this is not necessarily the rule. Another danger period occurs after the young have been removed from their mother at an age of six to eight weeks. Most breeders prefer healthy litters of two or three young because a healthy and robust female can handle these without much effort. Any breeder should be satisfied with that!

11. Mutations

Mutation breeding is a wide open and very interesting field. *Mutation* translated means *sudden change*. New colors are produced through inherited genetic changes that usually occur as a side effect of inbreeding. Sometime during the mid-1960's a mating of this kind set up by the American chinchilla breeder Larssen produced some very light blue young, which he called Saphire. These animals displayed the agouti pattern with a light blue undercoat, a blue-white band, and light blue clouding.

WHITE

In 1955 a white chinchilla male was born on the farm of the American breeder Wilson. This animal was the progeny of normal standard parents. It was not a true albino (i.e., with characteristic red eyes), but instead a distinctive mutation, the first of its type ever known to have occurred in chinchillas. This white buck entered the annals of chinchilla history designated as 44R-B17 (44R = establishment number, B = year designation for 1955, 17 = litter number). Its offspring are known as Wilson Whites.

Some years went by until the first white chinchillas reached the market, and because of their rarity they

A white chinchilla; white is just one of the many different color varieties developed by breeders over the course of time.

were traded at very high prices. At that time it was generally believed that mating a white buck with off-colored standards would improve the color of the standard progeny. This was subsequently proven to be wrong.

Today white mutation chinchillas are cheaper than good quality standard animals. The whites have one fur characteristic that is well-defined and present in standards: density. Mating white with standard (one can use either the darkest or lightest females) produces 50% whites and 50% standards in the first generation. The whites are either pure white or white with black guard hairs. The pelt is uniformly white and does not display the characteristic agouti pattern of normal chinchilla undercoats.

Matings of whites with standards may also give silver white and platinum animals. Both of these types will show the agouti pattern again. The silver animals have a silver-gray undercoat, a white band, and a silver-gray veil. The platinum chinchillas have a light blue undercoat, bluish white band, and a bluish clouding. So-called "pied" animals can also occur, primarily from matings of white bucks with off-colored females. The veil in pied animals is not uniform but instead patchy. Matings of white bucks with white females give young that are pure white, but they are not viable since they have inherited a lethal factor.

The fur trade is not particularly interested in white pelts, since these are indistinguishable from white rabbits' pelts. Yet the whites are of some importance for mutation breeding for the development of new colors. Here I must diverge and point out that mutation breeding requires a significantly higher breeding skill than for linebreeding. Only very experienced breeders should try their hand at this. Only these qualified breeders are in a position to do such pioneer work, since they have the necessary experience and patience and financial resources for experimentation.

BEIGE

In due course other mutations were developed. For a while beige mutations were very much in vogue. Matings between beige bucks and clear-blue standard females give light beige (pearl colored) and medium to dark beige shades (pastel colors). Mating beige with white produces cream colored progeny that are called Rose or Apricot. Here it is interesting to note that crosses between beige males and pied females produce uniform, pure cream colored progeny. Therefore, it can not be said that the "pied" condition is genetically passed on. Of course, the above-mentioned crosses also always produce a certain percentage of standard animals. Matings of beige with beige give either dark beige progeny or Rose animals unless the characteristics of other existing genetic features were already dominant. Whites or standards are also possible.

BLACKS

Much discussed recently are the black mutations called Black Velvet. They were bred and developed in 1956 by the American breeder Gunning. The fur on these animals has a black undercoat, a very narrow gray-white band, jet-black veil, and a very high density. Black Velvet is of considerable significance for chinchilla breeding, since its superb fur density, clouding (veil) with continuous strands, and fur pattern are genetically passed on to a large extent. Mated with clear-colored standards, it produces the most beautiful mutation ever seen in chinchillas, the Blue Black Velvet. Matings of black bucks with females from other mutations have produced Saphire Velvets, Pastel Velvets, and Brown Velvets.

Some years ago I obtained in my own facility two chocolate-brown bucks from a linebreeding mating. The fur of these animals had a deep dark brown undercoat, light brown band, and black-brown veil; the abdomen was also brown. Neither one of these bucks produced any progeny since both had a lethal factor.

Because chinchillas used as pets are graded on general appearance, health, and personality rather than just their pelt quality, the growing number of pet chinchillas already represents a variety of colors seldom preserved in fur farms. To a pet owner a white chinchilla is very attractive and desirable, while to a fur producer whites are weak and do not sell well. The pet fancy may be the only hope of preserving odd colors that may hold the key to producing even more unusual colors and patterns.

12. Selective Breeding

QUALITY IMPROVEMENT

In animal production it is not only important to maintain quality but also to improve it further. Improving quality is done by means of selective breeding. Without continuous selection there can be no quality improvement and no progress. Many a breeder has started out with high quality animals but then was only interested in large numbers of progeny without being selective in regard to quality. This inevitably resulted in a decline in the quality of the chinchillas produced; it was essentially a step backward.

Breeding selection as it concerns commercially raised chins has been for the following characteristics: 1) fur characters, such as purity of color, density, silkiness, hairs, clouding (veil), and fur pattern; 2) breeding characteristics in males, such as vitality, willingness to mate and excellent heredity; 3) in females: excellent littering characteristics (regular large litters), good milk production, ability to raise the young, body size and structure (shape and form); and 4) in males and females: excellent health and condition, resistance against diseases, compatibility and quiet disposition (no nervousness).

Breeding of pet quality animals will tend to concentrate on factors 3 and 4. The small number of specimens likely to be available to a pet breeder is usually too small to have any effect on overall selection for any character, as selective breeding programs require large numbers of offspring bred over many generations.

How can breeding be improved? First of all, the large-scale breeder must make sure that his breeding stock consists of at least 20 females, either from his own production or obtained through purchase. Following a close quality screening and evaluation of the entire breeding stock and progeny, respectively, those females of the same color are placed together into polygamous breeding groups together with the best available breeding bucks. Here the breeder has to make sure that the male's color class is at least one step (shade) darker than the females'. That is, one mates, for instance, medium dark females with dark or very dark bucks and dark females only with very dark bucks. (Fur producers have found that dark pelts always are preferred to light pelts and sell at higher prices.) The official evaluation certificate should state the color class. The female offspring from such matings should also be officially examined and evaluated and then placed into new groups with very dark bucks from different blood lines. Proper use of a high quality buck is decisive for improving breeding quality. Such a buck must not only possess good fur and breeding characteristics, he must also be able to pass these on to his progeny.

A good male can be used for up to five years. Its successors should be closely scrutinized and evaluated. First-class males that have a clear color, excellent fur density, compact body shape, and—especially—an extensive, dense clouding (veil) should be mated with females from different blood lines. Males that do not conform to these standards should not be bred.

There is an essential tool that is absolutely mandatory in selective breeding—this is maintaining a stud book with the exact details on males and females and their progeny. This process of breed improvement and selection is a continuous one. Only this will enable breeders to be competitive and produce quality animals.

LINEBREEDING

The breeder must proceed with sensitivity and understanding for the slow transformation and influence of the living animal in his initial attempts to improve the breeding characteristics of his stock. A more difficult procedure—to improve the overall quality of his stock—is through linebreeding. Generally this refers to a breeding method whereby over several generations certain characteristics are being continuously being selected for. The underlying principle of this method is to approach and obtain as closely as possible the characteristics of the ancestral male. There are various ways to organize a linebreeding program for chinchillas. Here I would like to give you an example from my own experience of how to set up linebreeding relatively easily.

Before I get into the subject proper, I have to point out the following. In order to improve our breeding stock we need suitable bucks, which can only be obtained through linebreeding. As a word of caution though: linebreeding as such tends to be associated with risks and can, in fact, produce exactly the opposite result of what is intended. Breeders who wish to get involved with such experiments must own a sufficiently large breeding stock (at least 50 chins) before they should decide to embark on such a venture. Breeders are warned against pursuing linebreeding indiscriminately, as experienced breeders know that normal breeding with selected chinchillas can also be very stimulating.

Linebreeding must be embarked upon with much thought and with only a small percentage of the entire animal stock available. I started out with a single polygamous group that consisted of one 15 A 3' (WGS classification) buck, tattoo AM-F13 (AM = establishment symbol, F13 = letter indicating year of birth + litter number), and four females (two 14 A and two 15 A). The male was dark blue, the females medium dark and dark, and all were progeny from excellent parental stock.

The first litters from this group produced six males and four females. Those males that were of unsuitable color and skin quality were culled; the others were used for further breeding. I used only two of the young females in further linebreeding, those that were identical to their father in coloration. I removed the other two young females and their respective mother from the group and mated them elsewhere.

Now the group consisted of the original male, two old females, and two young females (the daughters of the former). In order to have more young females available for this buck, I added to this group three additional females that had already produced a litter. Now this group consisted of the 15 A male and seven females. The selected young females (daughters) were, when sexually mature, mated with their father. This then started the first segment of linebreeding.

THE F1 GENERATION

After an impatiently endured waiting period of six months, the two young females produced a total of two males and one female. With these births the F1 generation had been reached. The males and the female were of a very attractive dark blue color, but in form and shape there were some differences. Particularly noticeable was the dark, short-haired underside of the tail, which was darker than in normal standard animals.

The young developed normally but displayed differences in guard hairs. In both juvenile males the guard hairs were denser than in their father, and in the young female they were sparser than in her father. These denser hairs also gave greater elasticity and silkiness. This confirmed that I had obtained not only better color but that there was also already an improvement in fur quality.

In terms of growth and shape the young males still exhibited the slight Costina trait of their father, while the young female was more like the broad-headed, large La Plata type of its mother. (Costina and La Plata are two major body types in chinchillas.)

In the meantime, the mothers of the young females that remained in the linebreeding program (those which had already produced the F1 generation) gave birth to an additional four young, two males and two females. From these I was able to use only a single female for continued linebreeding, since the other three did not conform to the required color prerequisites.

The three breeding females when mated with the original male of the breeding group produced a total of three young, all males. Although these females had previously produced litters of two and three, they failed almost completely with the new male. In other words, a different mating arrangement had detrimental effects on the number of progeny. There may well be exceptions, yet I learned my lesson from this and I have never attempted anything like it again.

The young males from those females that had disappointed me were later given a rating of 15 A, but I did not follow up on their respective breeding performances. I removed those three females from the group again and returned them to their former polygamous groups. Yet one was already pregnant again and gave birth to a female that I used later on in linebreeding. The two other females produced—after a pause of about nine to ten months—their usual litters of two and three young.

For the start of the next step in linebreeding I had—after two years—the two original females with four daughters on hand. The F1 generation, which consisted of two bucks and females, had meanwhile grown up and I looked forward to their evaluation with eager anticipation. One of the bucks was given a 15 A 4′ in background coloration, elasticity, guard hair cover, and body structure, while the other got a 15 A 3′ in background coloration, elasticity, and guard hair cover, just like their father. I designated the first buck (with 4 A′) as the main stud of a new linebreeding group; he was mated up with four 15 A standard females.

KEEPING A STUD BOOK

Here it may be relevant to point out that proper linebreeding is really not possible at all without keeping a detailed stud book. After all, a stud book is already an essential tool for normal chinchilla breeding. Moreover, it is strongly recommended that breeders without sufficient knowledge about fur characteristics have their animals evaluated before starting linebreeding; the same must be done with the progeny. This requirement is supported by my comments above. It requires the help of an experienced and neutral judge for the novice breeder to start up and maintain linebreeding.

From this point on my comments refer only to a single line of the first linebreeding group. Including the other lines from the same original group would make this discussion too cumbersome. Clarity and lucidity would suffer and this discussion would become confusing and possibly lead to mistakes.

Therefore, I will confine myself to the ancestral stud male AM-F13 and one of his females with the tattoo (identification symbol) AM-F8. This mating gave rise to female AM-H9, which was—as mentioned above—the only useful female. This particular female, AM-H9, was then mated to her father, AM-F13. The useful female offspring from the F1 generation (progeny of father and daughter) was given the tattoo AM-J17(F1) and obtained a rating of 15 A 4'. The other siblings were placed with other standard groups because they did not reach the rating of their parents, although they were otherwise attractive animals.

THE F2 GENERATION

After female AM-J17(F1) had reached sexual maturity she was mated with the ancestral stud male AM-F13, which started me on the path toward the F2 generation. Within six months female J17(F1) had her first litter with two young, one of each sex. With this litter the F2 generation had been reached.

How did these young compare in terms of their appearance? The young male looked like its father in terms of color and elasticity, but its guard hair cover was denser. Morphologically it was less developed. On the other hand, his sister was poorer than her mother, but morphologically it was larger than its brother.

This buck, which was given the identifying number AM-K7, was evaluated at an age of 13 months, when it obtained a rating of 15 A 5'; the A 5' was given for fur density. For the first time there was also an improvement in the veil (clouding) and fur pattern. Clouding extended far ventrally along the shoulders, sides and flanks and formed a distinct delineation toward the abdomen, which was quite narrow and of white coloration.

The buck AM-K7(F2) was then mated to the most attractive linebred female from another line. There was no genetic relationship between these animals. During the subsequent period this buck transferred its superior characteristics in color, density, clouding, elasticity, silkiness, fur pattern, and guard hair cover to about 40% of its progeny.

THE F3 GENERATION

The sister of the above-mentioned buck (AM-K7) with tattoo AM-K8(F2) was mated with the ancestral stud male AM-F13. This was the start of the F3 generation. The first litter—three young, two females and one male—was of above average quality; on the other hand the second (fall) litter was a total disaster. The two young, both males, did not even reach the rating of 12 A. The band had wrong colors on the head and neck. Moreover, growth deteriorated rapidly, which meant that these animals at an age of 12 months resembled four-month-old animals.

On the basis of these results I had to reach a decision whether matings should be continued or discontinued. Since the first litter produced above-average animals (the male obtained a 15 A 6′!), I decided on a renewed mating after a pause of six months. This produced one litter of two young (male and female), where the male once again was of superior quality while the female reached only 14 A; it had fallen behind in growth.

The result to that point was 50:50, and I continued breeding.

THE F4 GENERATION

Once again I crossed the young female AM-L40(F3) with the ancestral stud F13. This female produced—during the F4 generation—high quality progeny again, but only one young per litter. I was satisfied with that result, because the ten progeny bucks included two with 15 A 8′, four between 15 A 6′ and A 7′, and the other ones just barely below that level.

I felt that further incrossing would not be advisable, because I had obtained similar results in other linebreeding groups. Instead I started incrosses of the young F4 females with large-bodied bucks from different blood lines. I hope that with these comments I have thoroughly clarified the concept of F1, F2, F3, and F4 generations in linebreeding.

The purpose and advantages of linebreeding are obvious. In terms of color one obtains better animals of more even quality, with a greater density and silkiness, better clouding, and a more even fur pattern. In terms of fur production this is of greatest importance.

My comments also demonstrate that linebreeding can lead to a concentration of inferior characteristics. Such animals must be immediately eliminated. Generally speaking, one can expect losses of up to 50%. This refers not only to litter mortalities but also to deterioration of quality. Moreover, linebred animals are usually weak and have tendencies toward fur biting and sterility. These risks have to be accepted, and every breeder will have to know how far he wants to go in continuing a particular genetic line.